Happy 15th Birthday
Jeff !
Someday your name will be
in a book like this !!!
Love,
Mom

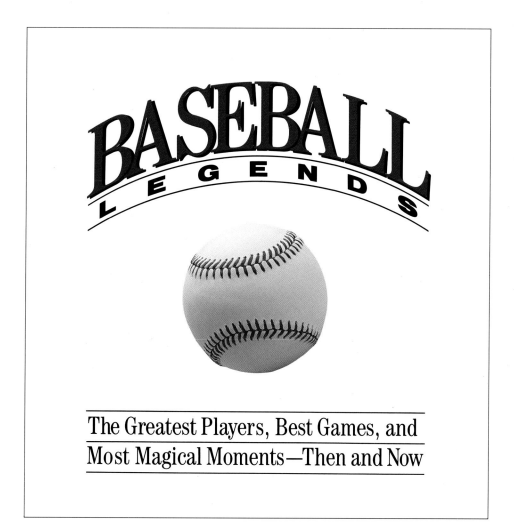

# BASEBALL LEGENDS

The Greatest Players, Best Games, and
Most Magical Moments—Then and Now

COURAGE BOOKS

An Imprint of
RUNNING PRESS
Philadelphia, Pennsylvania

**A FRIEDMAN GROUP BOOK**

Copyright © 1988, 1993 by Michael Friedman Publishing Group, Inc.

9   8   7   6   5   4   3   2   1

Digit on the right indicates the number of this printing.

Library of Congress Cataloging-in-Publication number 92-054934

ISBN 1-56138-266-3

*BASEBALL LEGENDS*
*The Greatest Players, Best Games, and Most Magical Moments—Then and Now*
was prepared and produced by
Michael Friedman Publishing Group, Inc.
15 West 26th Street
New York, New York 10010

Editor: Bruce Lubin
Art Director: Mary Moriarty
Designer: Rod Gonzalez
Photography Editor: Christine Cancelli
Cover Design: Toby Schmidt

Typeset by Classic Type, Inc.
Color separations by South Sea Graphic Arts Company Ltd.
Printed in Hong Kong by Leefung-Asco Printers Ltd.

Published by Courage Books
An imprint of
**Running Press Book Publishers**
125 South Twenty-second Street
Philadelphia, Pennsylvania 19103

## DEDICATION:

For my parents, Suzanne and Greg, who still labor under the
impression that the Red Sox play football.

---

## ACKNOWLEDGMENTS:

Thanks to those whose help made this book a reality: Claire Smith,
the fine baseball writer for the Hartford Courant; Henry Gola, a
terrific shortstop with a deep respect for the game; the fanatics at
the Elias Sports Bureau; editor Bruce Lubin of the Michael
Friedman Publishing Group; Mrs. Pat Kelly and Mr. Thomas
Heitz, photo manager and librarian at Cooperstown; photo
researcher Chris Cancelli; Joseph Reichler, whose *Baseball
Encyclopedia* is probably the only place to discover that Pumpsi
Green (.246 lifetime batting average) was born Elijah Jerry Green.

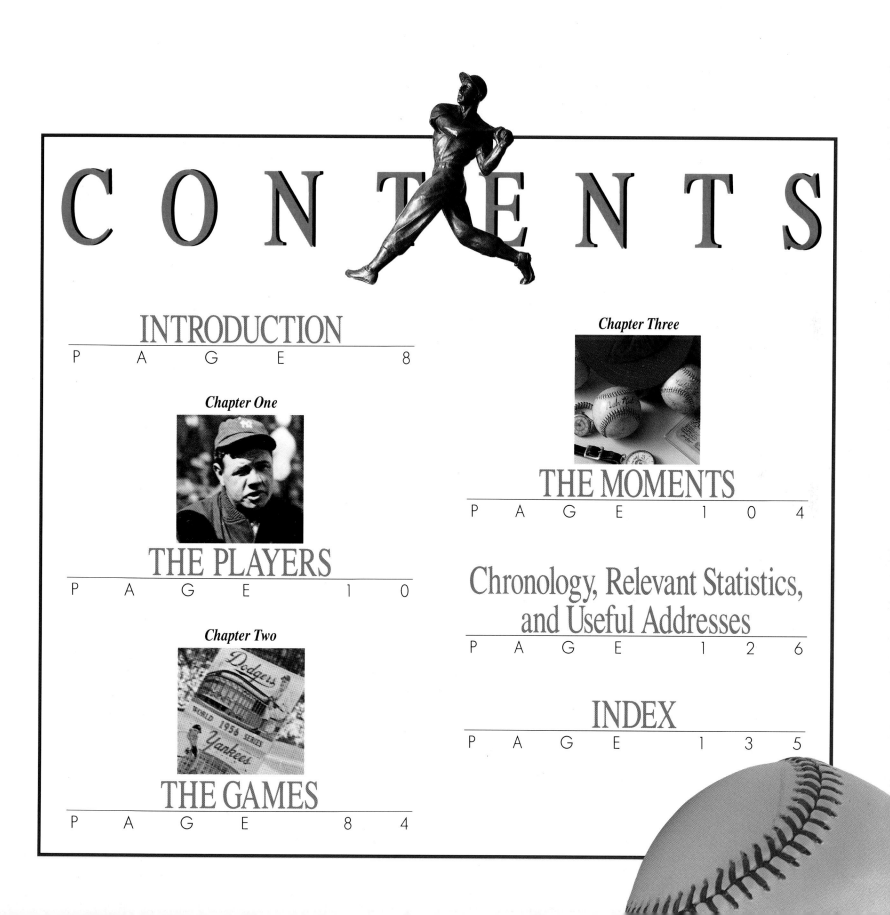

# C O N T E N T S

# Introduction

*Baseball enjoys a grip on nostalgia like no other sport. Although the world has changed over the last 100 years, baseball remains the same.*

**B**aseball's timeless nature is no accident. When Alexander J. Cartwright organized the first game of baseball on June 19, 1846 in Hoboken, New Jersey, he didn't depend on a clock. Fortunately, through the years, those who oversaw the evolution of the game didn't tamper with the beautiful symmetry. Baseball is the only major sport that doesn't limit itself within the framework of time, and perhaps as a result, its appeal transcends all other sports.

Above all, baseball is a game for open air and sunshine, as the Chicago Cubs discovered in 1988. On August 8, the lights came on at Wrigley Field for the first time in the history of the stadium. The Cubbies, playing under a $5 million set of new lights, were ahead 3-1 in the fourth inning. And then the heavens opened, and the rain began to fall. "It looked like the good Lord said, 'I'm going to show you why Wrigley Field has always been in the daylight,'" said Chicago pitcher Rick Sutcliffe. The next night, the Cubs beat the New York Mets 6-4 in Wrigley's first official night game.

Still, a summer afternoon in the bleachers at Wrigley can be a mystical experience. And later in the season, on a crisp October night, the urgency of a World Series can suspend a city, not to mention an entire nation. Baseball, of course, is forever, which is why little boys have been trading baseball cards since the turn of the century. The faces change, but the game remains the same: vibrant and at once intellectual and visceral, which is why some little boys never grow up.

There are no penalties in baseball, save for taking a called third strike with two out in the bottom of the ninth. The fouls in baseball are not indiscretions committed with malice—as happens in basketball—but merely unsuccessful attempts to place the ball in fair territory. Fair or foul. There isn't much of a gray area there. And might does not necessarily make right in this poetic game. No, baseball is a fanfare for the common man of uncommon abilities, whose only tools are a wooden bat, leather glove, and ball made of animal hide and thread. It isn't hard to relate to a 5-foot-9 shortstop who wears a cap, as opposed to a hulking 290-pound defensive tackle who grunts behind a menacing helmet.

*An autographed baseball stays with a youngster forever. Even when he's seventy years old.*

Baseball endures. St. Louis Browns owner, Bill Veeck—baseball's best salesman—suited up Eddie Gaedel on August 18, 1951. Gaedel, a midget wearing the number 1/8 for the Browns, walked on four straight pitches. Baseball, an institution that has always understood the difference between entertainment and dubious enterprise, didn't allow it to happen again. Controversial Oakland owner Charlie O. Finley tried to introduce Day-Glo orange baseballs, and he, too, was given the thumb. One suspects that three strikes will always make an out.

And while labor disputes linger and salaries continue to spiral out of the realm of believability (the very best players exceed salaries of $5 million a year for playing a game), baseball is still one of the best escapes from this hopelessly complicated world. A day at the ballpark with a hot dog and an ice-cold beer is truly rejuvenating. Good therapy never came cheaper.

Baseball's greatest gift is its unfailing flexibility. Nearly everything is defensible, in one way or another. To hit and run or play it safe? Do you let the number nine hitter swing away with a three-ball, one-strike count? Is a squeeze play advisable in this situation? Yes. And no. Depending on who is making the decision and who is making a judgment with the benefit of hindsight.

Much of baseball's attraction is based on historical arguments. Was Honus Wagner, the "Flying Dutchman" who played from 1897 to 1917 and averaged .329, a better shortstop than Larry Bowa, the modern-era player who led the National League in fielding percentage six times? Does Ty Cobb's best-ever .367 career batting average deserve an asterisk in the record book because he never played a 162-game schedule or a game under inadequate lights? Is Sandy Koufax, with 169 career victories, any less a pitcher than Gaylord Perry or Phil Niekro, who both achieved 300 wins in nearly twice as many games?

And thus the debates rage in barrooms and around kitchen tables. They probably always will. What follows are one fan's opinions.

# HANK AARON

*Although he hit only 13 homers his first full season in the Big Leagues, Hank Aaron averaged 34 home runs for each of the next 22 seasons.*

---

*Aaron's major league record of 6,856 total bases is 722 more than Stan Musial's second-place total.*

---

He is the first name in *The Baseball Encyclopedia* and the last name in home runs. He is, of course, Hank Louis Aaron, who leads the way alphabetically and by glorious example.

Aaron, economical and brilliantly consistent, endured for 24 years and broke many important slugging records. The 6-foot, 185-pound Mobile, Alabama right-hander passed Babe Ruth's cherished milestone of 714 home runs on April 4, 1974 and didn't stop until he reached 755, as imposing a number as there is in baseball. There are others: 2,297 runs batted in, 6,856 total bases, 1,477 extra-base hits—major-league records all.

Hammerin' Hank made 24 All-Star game appearances and compiled a marvelous .305 batting average. His muscular line drives led to two National League batting titles, something unusual for a player of such strength.

Aaron had left home at the age of seventeen with two dollars in his pocket, two sandwiches in his hand and two pairs of pants. His first train ride took him to the Indianapolis Clowns, a barnstorming team. The following year he became the shortstop for Eau Claire in the Northern League and batted .336, but hit only nine home runs. After a season at Jacksonville of the South Atlantic League (22 home runs), Aaron was ready to join the Milwaukee Braves. He was thrown into an uncertain outfield situation and came up swinging. The home runs (13) weren't there quite yet, but a .280 batting average and respectable runs batted in (69) and runs scored (58) offered a promising future.

No one was prepared for what followed. It wasn't that Aaron exploded on the scene, drawing the eyes of the baseball world; Willie Mays and Mickey Mantle were still the leading lights of the major leagues. No, Aaron started putting together one muscular season after another. First came his impressive 1957 effort: 44 home runs, 132 runs batted in, 118 runs scored, and a batting average of .322. Then, in 1963, Aaron produced nearly identical numbers: 44 home runs, 130 runs batted in, 121 runs scored, and a .319 average. Such was his greatest gift: To reproduce that magnificent swing again and again.

Aaron never enjoyed a 50-home run season the way Ruth, Maris, Mantle, and Mays did, but he averaged 33 homers a year, and exactly 100 runs batted in. Only Ty Cobb produced more runs than Hank Aaron's 3,716.

When it was all over, Aaron had done it all. In 1957, he had won the league's Most Valuable Player award and hit three home runs as the Braves won the World Series. And because he is first in home runs by such a wide margin, Aaron's record is sure to last.

*It's a round ball and a round bat and
you've got to hit it square. No one was
squarer than Henry Aaron.*

## S T A T S

| YEAR | G | AB | H | 2B | 3B | HR | TB | R | RBI | BB | AVG |
|------|------|-------|------|-----|----|-----|------|------|------|------|------|
| 1954 | 122 | 468 | 131 | 27 | 6 | 13 | 209 | 58 | 69 | 28 | .280 |
| 1955 | 153 | 602 | 189 | 37 | 9 | 27 | 325 | 105 | 106 | 49 | .314 |
| 1956 | 153 | 609 | 200 | 34 | 14 | 26 | 340 | 106 | 92 | 37 | .328 |
| 1957 | 151 | 615 | 198 | 27 | 6 | 44 | 369 | 118 | 132 | 57 | .322 |
| 1958 | 153 | 601 | 196 | 34 | 4 | 30 | 328 | 109 | 95 | 59 | .326 |
| 1959 | 154 | 629 | 223 | 46 | 7 | 39 | 400 | 116 | 123 | 51 | .355 |
| 1960 | 153 | 590 | 172 | 20 | 11 | 40 | 334 | 102 | 126 | 60 | .292 |
| 1961 | 155 | 603 | 197 | 39 | 10 | 34 | 358 | 115 | 120 | 56 | .327 |
| 1962 | 156 | 592 | 191 | 28 | 6 | 45 | 366 | 127 | 128 | 66 | .323 |
| 1963 | 161 | 631 | 201 | 29 | 4 | 44 | 370 | 121 | 130 | 78 | .319 |
| 1964 | 145 | 570 | 187 | 30 | 2 | 24 | 293 | 103 | 95 | 62 | .328 |
| 1965 | 150 | 570 | 181 | 40 | 1 | 32 | 319 | 109 | 89 | 60 | .318 |
| 1966 | 158 | 603 | 168 | 23 | 1 | 44 | 325 | 117 | 127 | 76 | .279 |
| 1967 | 155 | 600 | 184 | 37 | 3 | 39 | 344 | 113 | 109 | 63 | .307 |
| 1968 | 160 | 606 | 174 | 33 | 4 | 29 | 302 | 84 | 86 | 64 | .287 |
| 1969 | 147 | 547 | 164 | 30 | 3 | 44 | 332 | 100 | 97 | 87 | .300 |
| 1970 | 150 | 516 | 154 | 26 | 1 | 38 | 296 | 103 | 118 | 74 | .298 |
| 1971 | 139 | 495 | 162 | 22 | 3 | 47 | 331 | 95 | 118 | 71 | .327 |
| 1972 | 129 | 449 | 119 | 10 | 0 | 34 | 231 | 75 | 77 | 92 | .265 |
| 1973 | 120 | 392 | 118 | 12 | 1 | 40 | 232 | 84 | 96 | 68 | .301 |
| 1974 | 112 | 340 | 91 | 16 | 0 | 20 | 167 | 47 | 69 | 39 | .268 |
| 1975 | 137 | 465 | 109 | 16 | 2 | 12 | 165 | 45 | 60 | 70 | .234 |
| 1976 | 85 | 271 | 62 | 8 | 0 | 10 | 100 | 22 | 35 | 35 | .229 |
| **TOTAL** | **3298** | **12364** | **3771** | **624** | **98** | **755** | **6856** | **2174** | **2297** | **1402** | **.305** |

# JOHNNY BENCH

*Bench won 10 consecutive Rawlings Gold Glove awards as the National League's best defensive catcher.*

Catching is a dirty job, which is why there are so few good catchers. Johnny Lee Bench, who was born in 1947 in Oklahoma City, Oklahoma, might have been the best.

When Bench was enshrined at Cooperstown in 1989, he became only the nineteenth player in history to gain entry to the Hall of Fame in his first year of eligibility. After a century of baseball, only two players (Ty Cobb and Hank Aaron) received a higher percentage of votes (96.4) than Bench did from the Baseball Writers Association of America.

His offensive statistics were outstanding. In 17 seasons, from 1967 to 1983, Bench hit 389 home runs and drove in 1,376 runs. He also managed a total of 2,048 hits.

But Bench's defensive contributions were even greater. Before Bench, catchers squatted behind the plate and used both hands to catch the ball. Bench revolutionized the position, protecting his throwing hand behind his back. Not only did this prevent hand injuries, which were commonplace for catchers, but it also allowed him to stop balls in the dirt without losing his balance. In addition, Bench had a powerful arm that kept even good base runners on the defensive.

Above all, Bench was a master at calling a game. At the tender age of 20, he began han-

dling a veteran Cincinnati Reds pitching staff, with great success. The Reds went to the World Series four times in a seven-year span, and Bench might have been the main cog in the "Big Red Machine."

Bench's first full season in the major leagues was 1968, when he hit 15 home runs and batted .275. He was named the National League's Rookie of the Year. Two years later, in 1970, Bench had the best season of his career. He belted 45 home runs, drove in 148 runs, and hit .293. Still shy of his 23rd birthday, Bench was voted the National League's Most Valuable Player. Two seasons later he would earn the honor again with a league-leading 40 homers and 125 runs batted in. In 1974, he hit another 33 home runs and added a league-leading 129 runs batted in.

Typically, Bench was at his best under pressure. He was the 1976 World Series MVP, hitting two home runs, a triple and a double. Bench drove in six runs and hit .533 as the Reds won their second consecutive World Series championship.

In a span of 10 seasons, Bench knocked in a staggering 1,032 runs. When he finished his career, Bench left with a piece of history: of his 389 career home runs, 327 came as a catcher, the all-time record when he retired in 1983.

*Johnny Bench was not only an outstanding catcher (opposite page), but a tremendous batter (right) as well. He managed to revolutionize the catcher's stance while often leading his league in home runs and runs batted in.*

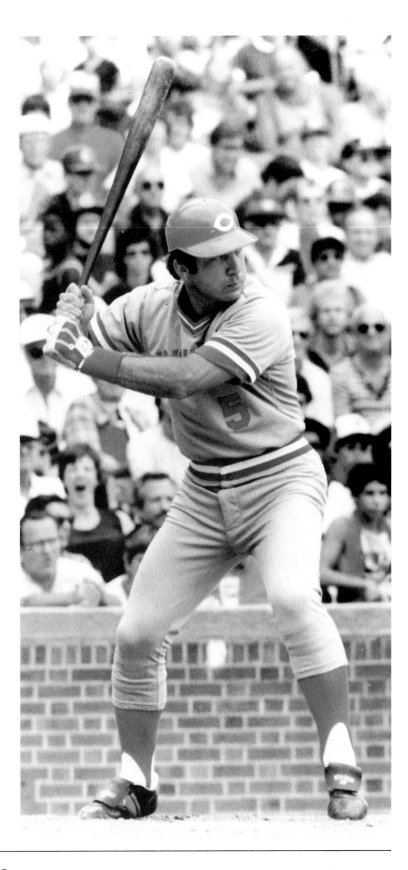

## S T A T S

| YEAR | G | AB | H | 2B | 3B | HR | TB | R | RBI | BB | AVG |
|------|-----|------|------|-----|----|-----|------|------|------|-----|------|
| 1967 | 26 | 86 | 14 | 3 | 1 | 1 | 22 | 7 | 6 | 5 | .163 |
| 1968 | 154 | 564 | 155 | 40 | 2 | 15 | 244 | 67 | 82 | 31 | .275 |
| 1969 | 148 | 532 | 156 | 23 | 1 | 26 | 259 | 83 | 90 | 49 | .293 |
| 1970 | 158 | 605 | 177 | 35 | 4 | 45 | 355 | 97 | 148 | 54 | .293 |
| 1971 | 149 | 562 | 134 | 19 | 2 | 27 | 238 | 80 | 61 | 49 | .238 |
| 1972 | 147 | 538 | 145 | 22 | 2 | 40 | 291 | 87 | 125 | 100 | .270 |
| 1973 | 152 | 557 | 141 | 17 | 3 | 25 | 239 | 83 | 104 | 83 | .253 |
| 1974 | 160 | 621 | 174 | 38 | 2 | 33 | 315 | 108 | 129 | 80 | .280 |
| 1975 | 142 | 530 | 150 | 39 | 1 | 28 | 275 | 83 | 110 | 65 | .283 |
| 1976 | 135 | 465 | 109 | 24 | 1 | 16 | 183 | 62 | 74 | 81 | .234 |
| 1977 | 142 | 494 | 136 | 34 | 2 | 31 | 267 | 67 | 109 | 58 | .275 |
| 1978 | 120 | 393 | 102 | 17 | 1 | 23 | 190 | 52 | 73 | 50 | .260 |
| 1979 | 130 | 464 | 128 | 19 | 0 | 22 | 213 | 73 | 80 | 67 | .276 |
| 1980 | 114 | 360 | 90 | 12 | 0 | 24 | 174 | 52 | 68 | 41 | .250 |
| 1981 | 52 | 178 | 55 | 8 | 0 | 8 | 87 | 14 | 25 | 17 | .309 |
| 1982 | 119 | 399 | 103 | 16 | 0 | 13 | 158 | 44 | 38 | 37 | .258 |
| 1983 | 110 | 310 | 79 | 15 | 2 | 12 | 134 | 32 | 54 | 24 | .255 |
| TOTAL | 2158 | 7658 | 2048 | 381 | 24 | 389 | 3644 | 1091 | 1376 | 891 | .267 |

*The cloud of dust tells the story: Ty Cobb could never stand still—not when there was a base to be stolen.*

*Note the intent gaze, the concentration.
It carried Ty Cobb to a lifetime batting
average of .367.*

## STATS

| EAR | G | AB | H | 2B | 3B | HR | TB | R | RBI | BB | AVG |
|---|---|---|---|---|---|---|---|---|---|---|---|
| 1905 | 41 | 150 | 36 | 6 | 0 | 1 | 45 | 19 | 15 | 10 | .240 |
| 1906 | 98 | 358 | 113 | 13 | 7 | 1 | 143 | 45 | 41 | 19 | .316 |
| 1907 | 150 | 605 | 212 | 29 | 15 | 5 | 286 | 97 | 116 | 24 | .350 |
| 1908 | 150 | 581 | 188 | 36 | 20 | 4 | 276 | 88 | 101 | 34 | .324 |
| 1909 | 156 | 573 | 216 | 33 | 10 | 9 | 296 | 116 | 115 | 48 | .377 |
| 1910 | 140 | 508 | 194 | 35 | 13 | 8 | 279 | 106 | 88 | 64 | .382 |
| 1911 | 146 | 591 | 248 | 47 | 24 | 8 | 367 | 147 | 144 | 44 | .420 |
| 1912 | 140 | 553 | 227 | 30 | 23 | 7 | 324 | 119 | 90 | 43 | .410 |
| 1913 | 122 | 428 | 167 | 18 | 16 | 4 | 229 | 70 | 67 | 58 | .390 |
| 1914 | 97 | 345 | 127 | 22 | 11 | 2 | 177 | 69 | 57 | 57 | .368 |
| 1915 | 156 | 563 | 208 | 31 | 13 | 3 | 274 | 144 | 99 | 118 | .369 |
| 1916 | 145 | 542 | 201 | 31 | 10 | 5 | 267 | 113 | 68 | 78 | .371 |
| 1917 | 152 | 588 | 225 | 44 | 23 | 7 | 336 | 107 | 102 | 61 | .383 |
| 1918 | 111 | 421 | 161 | 19 | 14 | 3 | 217 | 83 | 64 | 41 | .382 |
| 1919 | 124 | 497 | 191 | 36 | 13 | 1 | 256 | 92 | 70 | 38 | .384 |
| 1920 | 112 | 428 | 143 | 28 | 8 | 2 | 193 | 86 | 63 | 58 | .334 |
| 1921 | 128 | 507 | 197 | 37 | 16 | 12 | 302 | 124 | 101 | 56 | .389 |
| 1922 | 137 | 526 | 211 | 42 | 16 | 4 | 297 | 99 | 99 | 55 | .401 |
| 1923 | 145 | 556 | 189 | 40 | 7 | 6 | 261 | 103 | 88 | 66 | .340 |
| 1924 | 155 | 625 | 211 | 38 | 10 | 4 | 281 | 115 | 74 | 85 | .338 |
| 1925 | 121 | 415 | 157 | 31 | 12 | 12 | 248 | 97 | 102 | 65 | .378 |
| 1926 | 79 | 233 | 79 | 18 | 5 | 4 | 119 | 48 | 62 | 26 | .339 |
| 1927 | 133 | 490 | 175 | 32 | 7 | 5 | 236 | 104 | 93 | 67 | .357 |
| 1928 | 95 | 353 | 114 | 27 | 4 | 1 | 152 | 54 | 40 | 34 | .323 |
| TOTAL | 3033 | 11436 | 4190 | 723 | 297 | 118 | 5861 | 2245 | 1959 | 1249 | .367 |

*In DiMaggio's hands, the bat became almost a living thing. At times it looked like an extension of his arm.*

# JOE DiMAGGIO

*In only his second season (1937) DiMaggio hit 46 home runs to lead the major leagues.*

Surely, Joe DiMaggio was *the* baseball player's player. He was almost ethereal gliding around in center field at Yankee Stadium, and his graceful swing and follow-through appeared unconsciously efficient, like the man himself. "The Yankee Clipper," or "Joltin' Joe," if you prefer, was 6-foot-2, 193 pounds of smooth. It was all so easy. Too easy, some thought.

Forget the innate hitting ability for a moment. DiMaggio's teammates swear they never saw him make a mental error in thirteen years of playing for the Yankees. Thirteen years without a mistake in judgment? Well, once he attempted to stretch a single into a double and was called out against the Red Sox. The umpire, reportedly, admitted later that he had missed the call.

A skinny kid with a wide stance, he was discovered by Yankees' scout Bill Essick, who recommended in 1934 that General Manager Ed Barrow buy him from the San Francisco Seals. It cost New York only $25,000, five minor league players and an agreement to wait one season. DiMaggio, who finished the 1934 season with a .341 batting average, led the Seals to the Pacific Coast League title in 1935 with a .398 average, 34 home runs and 154 runs batted in. He was viewed as something of a savior when he arrived in New York. After all, the Yankees had won only one pennant in seven years.

DiMaggio delivered with a .323 average, 29 home runs, and 125 runs batted in, helping New York win the World Series for the first time since 1932. They played in the Fall Classic six times in DiMaggio's first seven seasons. He was a two-time batting champion, hitting .381 and .352 in 1939 and 1940. DiMaggio was named Most Valuable Player of the American League three times. His 361 career homers and 1,537 runs batted in were remarkable numbers for a player who lost three seasons to the war effort.

The thing people remember most, however, is DiMaggio's 56-game hitting streak, authored in 1941. It is recognized today as baseball's most difficult feat of all time. It is a record that may never be broken and is a testament to DiMaggio's remarkable talents, ability to persevere, and his unearthly powers of concentration. With Joe DiMaggio at the plate, though, it looked *so* easy.

Joe DiMaggio was a thin man, but somewhere he found the power to hit 361 career home runs. Timing, he said, was everything.

S T A T S

| YEAR | G | AB | H | 2B | 3B | HR | TB | R | RBI | BB | AVG |
|---|---|---|---|---|---|---|---|---|---|---|---|
| 1936 | 138 | 637 | 206 | 44 | 15 | 29 | 367 | 132 | 125 | 24 | .323 |
| 1937 | 151 | 621 | 215 | 35 | 15 | 46 | 418 | 151 | 167 | 64 | .346 |
| 1938 | 145 | 599 | 194 | 32 | 13 | 32 | 348 | 129 | 140 | 59 | .324 |
| 1939 | 120 | 462 | 176 | 32 | 6 | 30 | 310 | 108 | 126 | 52 | .381 |
| 1940 | 132 | 508 | 179 | 28 | 9 | 31 | 318 | 93 | 133 | 61 | .352 |
| 1941 | 139 | 541 | 193 | 43 | 11 | 30 | 348 | 122 | 125 | 76 | .357 |
| 1942 | 154 | 610 | 186 | 29 | 13 | 21 | 304 | 123 | 114 | 68 | .305 |
| 1946 | 132 | 503 | 146 | 20 | 8 | 25 | 257 | 81 | 95 | 59 | .290 |
| 1947 | 141 | 534 | 168 | 31 | 10 | 20 | 279 | 97 | 97 | 64 | .315 |
| 1948 | 153 | 594 | 190 | 26 | 11 | 39 | 355 | 110 | 155 | 67 | .320 |
| 1949 | 76 | 272 | 94 | 14 | 6 | 14 | 162 | 58 | 67 | 55 | .346 |
| 1950 | 139 | 525 | 158 | 33 | 10 | 32 | 307 | 114 | 122 | 80 | .301 |
| 1951 | 116 | 415 | 109 | 22 | 4 | 12 | 175 | 72 | 71 | 61 | .263 |
| TOTAL | 1736 | 6821 | 2214 | 389 | 131 | 361 | 3948 | 1390 | 1537 | 790 | .325 |

# LOU GEHRIG

*Gehrig hit 23 career grand slams, the major-league record. Babe Ruth managed only 16.*

When Wally Pipp wasn't up to playing first base for the New York Yankees one day in 1925, Lou Gehrig stepped into the lineup. He didn't come out for 2,130 games. Let there be no doubt why Gehrig was known as "The Iron Man." And yet, there are many more reasons why he is considered the greatest first baseman ever.

He broke the consecutive-game record of 1,307 set by L. Everett Scott, the shortstop for Boston and New York from 1914 to 1926. Gehrig's monstrous achievement remains a record today, and an unassailable one at that. Steve Garvey, playing for the Los Angeles Dodgers in the 1970s, put together a highly publicized run of 1,207 straight games. Garvey would have needed nearly six more seasons without a miss to pass Gehrig. But as breathtaking as that record of durability is, Gehrig's greatest contributions to the Yankees came from his bat.

Henry Louis Gehrig was born in New York, attended Columbia University, and in 1923, at the age of 20, found himself playing for the Yankees. Along with Babe Ruth, Gehrig formed baseball's most formidable and celebrated one-two punch. In 1927, Ruth, Gehrig, Bob Meusel, and Tony Lazzeri formed the middle of the lineup known as "Murderers' Row." That Yankees team won 100 games and swept Pittsburgh 4-0 in the World Series.

There may never have been a better team, and Gehrig was at the heart of it. In the American League that year, Ruth hit his magnificent 60 home runs, but Gehrig came in an impressive second with 47. Lazzeri's 18 were good for third, which says something about Ruth and Gehrig's dominance. Gehrig edged Ruth in the RBI department, 175-164, and in total bases, 447-417. Ruth and Gehrig were also one-two in runs scored, slugging percentage, and walks.

Gehrig hit .373 that year and average .340 for his 17-year career. His consistent power echoed his ability to play every day. For 13 straight seasons, Gehrig drove in more than 100 runs. He led the league five times in that category and finished his career with 1,991, a figure only Ruth and Hank Aaron surpassed. Three of the best six season RBI totals belong to Gehrig. And he scored 1,888 runs, a total that also ranks among the very best efforts of all-time.

He was always on the leading edge. In 1932, Gehrig became the first 20th century player to hit four consecutive home runs in one game. His World Series performances were superb: in 34 games, Gehrig hit 10 home runs, knocked in 35 runs, scored 30, and batted .361. It doesn't get much better than that. Durable numbers, to be sure.

*Back in his Ivy League days at Columbia, no one could have predicted that Lou Gehrig would have become such a phenomenal superstar.*

S · T · A · T · S

| YEAR | G | AB | H | 2B | 3B | HR | TB | R | RBI | BB | AVG |
|-------|------|------|------|-----|-----|-----|------|------|------|------|------|
| 1923 | 13 | 26 | 11 | 4 | 1 | 1 | 20 | 6 | 9 | 2 | .423 |
| 1924 | 10 | 12 | 6 | 1 | 0 | 0 | 7 | 2 | 6 | 1 | .500 |
| 1925 | 126 | 437 | 129 | 23 | 10 | 20 | 232 | 73 | 68 | 46 | .295 |
| 1926 | 155 | 572 | 179 | 47 | 20 | 16 | 314 | 135 | 107 | 105 | .313 |
| 1927 | 155 | 584 | 218 | 52 | 18 | 47 | 447 | 149 | 175 | 109 | .373 |
| 1928 | 154 | 562 | 210 | 47 | 13 | 27 | 364 | 139 | 142 | 95 | .374 |
| 1929 | 154 | 553 | 166 | 33 | 9 | 35 | 322 | 127 | 126 | 122 | .300 |
| 1930 | 154 | 581 | 220 | 42 | 17 | 41 | 419 | 143 | 174 | 101 | .379 |
| 1931 | 155 | 619 | 211 | 31 | 15 | 46 | 410 | 163 | 184 | 117 | .341 |
| 1932 | 156 | 596 | 208 | 42 | 9 | 34 | 370 | 138 | 151 | 108 | .349 |
| 1933 | 152 | 593 | 198 | 41 | 12 | 32 | 359 | 138 | 139 | 92 | .334 |
| 1934 | 154 | 579 | 210 | 40 | 6 | 49 | 409 | 128 | 165 | 109 | .363 |
| 1935 | 149 | 535 | 176 | 26 | 10 | 30 | 312 | 125 | 119 | 132 | .329 |
| 1936 | 155 | 579 | 205 | 37 | 7 | 49 | 403 | 167 | 152 | 130 | .354 |
| 1937 | 157 | 569 | 200 | 37 | 9 | 37 | 366 | 138 | 159 | 127 | .351 |
| 1938 | 157 | 576 | 170 | 32 | 6 | 29 | 301 | 115 | 114 | 107 | .295 |
| 1939 | 8 | 28 | 4 | 0 | 0 | 0 | 4 | 2 | 1 | 5 | .143 |
| TOTAL | 2164 | 8001 | 2721 | 535 | 162 | 493 | 5059 | 1888 | 1991 | 1508 | .340 |

Lou Gehrig was baseball's "Iron Man."
For 2,130 games he never took a break.

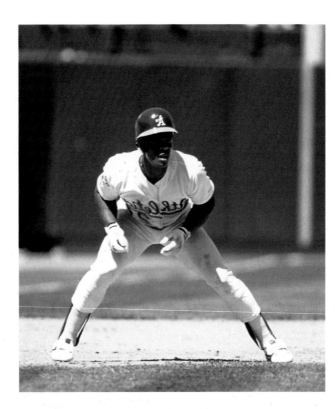

*Ricky Henderson's astonishing and unassailable record number of stolen bases is the result of a rare combination of lightning speed, a fearless approach, and the ability to accurately forecast a given play.*

# RICKY HENDERSON

*In the 12 seasons between 1980 and 1991, Henderson led the American League in stolen bases 11 times.*

Ricky Henderson inched off second base, eyed Yankees pitcher Tim Leary, and just as Leary committed himself to the plate, the muscular 5-foot-10, 195-pound athlete took off. He had guessed correctly; it was a slow change-up. Leaning forward slightly as he ran, Henderson gained momentum and threw himself headfirst into third base. He beat catcher Matt Nokes' one-hop throw easily. From a squat, Henderson called for a timeout, made the sign of the cross, rose, and wrenched the base from its mooring.

It took only five seconds; but it was a moment for all time. On May 1, 1991, in front of his home crowd, the gifted Oakland Athletics outfielder had just stolen his 939th base, eclipsing the long-held record of Lou Brock. Appropriately, it was Brock who presented Henderson with a plaque to commemorate the momentous event. And it was Brock's achievement that put Henderson's awesome feat in perspective. Brock had set the record in a 19-year career from 1961 to 1979, and Henderson broke it in seven fewer seasons, 1,001 fewer games, and 91 fewer attempts.

Going into the 1992 season at the age of 33, Henderson had pushed his record to 994 stolen bases. His 1991 total of 58 led the American League and placed him third in the major leagues—and that was an off year for Henderson.

He was born in 1958 in Chicago, Illinois, and after a four-year tour in the minor leagues (in such garden spots as Boise, Modesto, Jersey City, and Ogden), Henderson was promoted to the A's. He had already racked up 249 stolen bases in less than four seasons but, amazingly, that ratio would increase in the majors. In 89 games in 1979, Henderson stole 33 bases and hit .274. He had blinding speed, to be sure, but Henderson also had the rare ability to study pitchers, to read their intentions. He had a discriminating eye at the plate that allowed him to draw walks; you can't steal, after all, if you don't reach base. Henderson was also willing to hurl himself through the air and put himself through the daily pounding that consistent base stealing demands.

Henderson broke through in his first full season in Oakland. In 1980, he swiped an even 100 bases and hit .303. Two years later, the "Man of Steal" set the single season standard for base stealing, recording a phenomenal 130 steals. That shattered the previous mark of 118, set by Brock in 1974. After a five-year stint with the New York Yankees, Henderson returned to Oakland where he continued to run at will. He also helped the A's to a World Series victory in 1989, stealing eight bases in a four-game sweep of the San Francisco Giants. In 1990, Henderson was the American League's Most Valuable Player.

The stolen-base mark is a record that may stand longer than Brock's. After he became the all-time leading base stealer, Henderson was asked if he could put the record out of reach. "I don't know what out of reach is," Henderson said. "Nine hundred was once out of sight. I know I can steal 1,200."

| YEAR | G | AB | H | 2B | 3B | HR | TB | R | RBI | BB | SB | AVG |
|---|---|---|---|---|---|---|---|---|---|---|---|---|
| 1979 | 89 | 351 | 96 | 13 | 3 | 1 | 118 | 49 | 26 | 34 | 33 | .274 |
| 1980 | 158 | 591 | 179 | 22 | 4 | 9 | 236 | 111 | 53 | 117 | 100 | .303 |
| 1981 | 108 | 433 | 135 | 18 | 7 | 6 | 185 | 88 | 35 | 84 | 56 | .319 |
| 1982 | 149 | 536 | 143 | 24 | 4 | 10 | 205 | 119 | 51 | 118 | 130 | .267 |
| 1983 | 145 | 513 | 150 | 25 | 7 | 9 | 216 | 105 | 48 | 103 | 108 | .292 |
| 1984 | 142 | 502 | 147 | 27 | 4 | 16 | 230 | 113 | 58 | 88 | 66 | .293 |
| 1985 | 143 | 547 | 172 | 28 | 5 | 24 | 282 | 146 | 72 | 99 | 80 | .314 |
| 1986 | 153 | 608 | 160 | 31 | 5 | 28 | 285 | 130 | 74 | 89 | 87 | .263 |
| 1987 | 90 | 358 | 104 | 17 | 3 | 17 | 178 | 78 | 37 | 80 | 41 | .291 |
| 1988 | 140 | 554 | 169 | 30 | 2 | 6 | 221 | 118 | 50 | 82 | 93 | .305 |
| 1989NY | 65 | 235 | 58 | 13 | 1 | 3 | 82 | 41 | 22 | 56 | 25 | .247 |
| OAK | 85 | 306 | 90 | 13 | 2 | 9 | 134 | 72 | 35 | 70 | 52 | .294 |
| 1990 | 136 | 489 | 159 | 33 | 3 | 28 | 282 | 119 | 61 | 97 | 65 | .326 |
| 1991 | 134 | 470 | 126 | 17 | 1 | 18 | 199 | 105 | 57 | 98 | 58 | .268 |
| TOTAL | 1742 | 8483 | 1888 | 311 | 51 | 184 | 2853 | 1395 | 679 | 1215 | 994 | .281 |

*Reggie. He was a single-name enterprise who was truly global in scope. Just ask him.*

# REGGIE JACKSON

*Jackson holds the major league record with 2,584 strikeouts.*

Even when he missed, which was often enough, Reginald Martinez Jackson was exciting. His helmet would come off, and he would twist off balance in the batter's box. No matter, he had two more strikes. And it was Jackson's singular charisma that kept you in your seat wondering whether he was going to put one out or go down swinging.

Every goal has its price, and strikeouts (some 2,584) were a small piece of change considering the 563 home runs Jackson produced between 1967 and 1987. That places him sixth on the all-time list, ahead of gifted players like Mantle, Foxx, Schmidt, Williams, and Gehrig.

Jackson was born in Wyncote, Pennsylvania, and first rose to prominence at Arizona State University. The 6-foot, 206-pound outfielder was drafted second overall by the Kansas City Athletics in the 1966 free-agent draft, and one year later, he was playing with the big club. The A's moved to Oakland in 1967, and Jackson's first full year in the major leagues was notable for 29 home runs and also 171 strikeouts, a league-leading figure. That success-failure ratio would hold up for most of his career.

Reggie referred to himself as "the straw that stirs the drink," and he in turn stirred the hearts of a nation for the better part of two decades. Jackson, or "Mr. October," performed best when the bright lights were trained on him. His World Series record is unimpeachable.

Jackson hit .310 in his first two World Series when the A's defeated the New York Mets and

Los Angeles Dodgers in 1973 and 1974. Facing elimination in the sixth game against the Mets, the A's turned to Jackson. He knocked in Oakland's first two runs with doubles in the first and third innings, then singled and scored the third in a 3-1 victory. In the seventh game, Jackson and Bert Campaneris hit two-run home runs in the third inning of a game the A's would win 5-2.

Then, in 1977, Jackson offered one of the most memorable World Series performances in history. He had moved from Oakland to Baltimore in 1976 and to the Yankees a year later. Heading into Game Six with a 3-2 lead in the Series, New York was looking to finish off the Los Angeles Dodgers. Jackson, who had already homered twice in the Series, walked on four pitches from Burt Hooten the first time up. In the bottom of the fourth, Jackson took Hooten's first pitch over the right-field fence for a two-run homer. That gave the Yankees a 4-3 lead. The score was 7-3 after Jackson deposited Elias Sosa's first pitch even farther back than his first home run. Two swings, two home runs. And as Jackson came to the plate in the eighth inning, the New York fans were on their feet. Jackson stepped in against knuckleballer Charlie Hough, an unlikely home-run victim, but sure enough, the first pitch landed 450 feet away in the center-field bleachers. Jackson stopped to drink it all in while 90 feet away down the first-base line. Dodgers first baseman Steve Garvey was covertly applauding in his glove. Three swings, three home runs. History. Reggie.

# WALTER JOHNSON

*Johnson's 113 career shutouts are an all-time major league high; 38 of them were 1-0 complete games.*

Twenty victories in a season is the recognized standard of excellence for a pitcher. Most go an entire career failing to reach that milestone, while some of the better craftsmen manage the feat once or twice. Walter Perry "The Big Train" Johnson did it 12 times—for a losing team, the Washington Senators.

He went straight from the majors out of Humboldt, Kansas, a right-handed fireballer of 19. In 1910, his fourth season, Johnson won 25 games and lost 17. It was the beginning of a decade in which every season brought with it a 20-game season by Johnson. During that time, he won 264 games and lost 143. Those victories represented more than a third of the games the Senators managed to win during that time.

Johnson, at 6-foot-1, 200 pounds, was an imposing figure on the mound, though warm and affable off it. When he dropped to a three-quarters or sidearm motion he was pretty near impossible to hit. They didn't have radar guns in those days, but Johnson most certainly was in a class with Nolan Ryan, whose fastball has been clocked at over 100 miles an hour. And Johnson could put it anywhere he wanted.

Although Johnson developed a curveball that he was quite proud of, it was his fastball that left them swinging at air. Johnson struck out 3,506 batters, a record that stood for 54 years until Gaylord Perry broke it in 1983. In 1910, Johnson struck out 313 batters in 374 innings. He fanned 303 two years later while winning 32 games. In 1913, Johnson had the greatest year ever by a pitcher, going 36-7 with an earned run average of 1.09. He led the American League with 30 complete games, 12 shutouts, 243 strikeouts—and less than one walk per nine innings.

The list of accomplishments is staggering. Only Cy Young had more than Johnson's lifetime 416 victories. He once pitched 56 consecutive scoreless innings and in 1912 Johnson won 16 games in a row, a feat yet to be surpassed. And this was for a team that was generally awful. There was one, brief shining season, though.

In 1924, at age 37, Johnson pitched the Senators to the American League pennant. He was 23-7, though he had lost a yard on his fastball. He hadn't won 20 games for four seasons, but with Goose Goslin hitting .344 and knocking in 129 runs, Washington reached the World Series. Johnson lost his first two decisions to the New York Giants and came back with a masterful seventh-game effort. He pitched 12 innings, allowing only three runs, and was on base when Earl McNeely's grounder to third hit a pebble and took a wild hop over the head of Giants third baseman Fred Lindstrom. Muddy Ruel flew home with the winning run. It was Washington's first and only world championship.

A familiar story underlines Johnson's marvelous talent. Cleveland shortstop Ray Chapman once watched two fastballs sail past him at the plate, threw his bat down and headed for the dugout. "That's only strike two," hollered umpire Billy Evans.

"I know," Chapman said. "You can have the next one, it won't do me any good."

| YEAR | G | W | L | IP | SO | TBB | GS | CG | ShO | ERA |
|------|-----|-----|-----|------|------|------|-----|-----|-----|------|
| 1907 | 14 | 5 | 9 | 111 | 70 | 17 | 12 | 11 | 2 | 1.87 |
| 1908 | 36 | 14 | 14 | 257 | 160 | 53 | 29 | 23 | 6 | 1.64 |
| 1909 | 40 | 13 | 25 | 297 | 164 | 84 | 36 | 27 | 4 | 2.21 |
| 1910 | 45 | 25 | 17 | 373 | 313 | 76 | 42 | 38 | 8 | 1.35 |
| 1911 | 40 | 25 | 13 | 323 | 207 | 70 | 37 | 36 | 6 | 1.89 |
| 1912 | 50 | 32 | 12 | 368 | 303 | 76 | 37 | 34 | 7 | 1.39 |
| 1913 | 47 | 36 | 7 | 346 | 243 | 38 | 36 | 30 | 12 | 1.09 |
| 1914 | 51 | 28 | 18 | 372 | 225 | 74 | 40 | 33 | 10 | 1.72 |
| 1915 | 47 | 27 | 13 | 337 | 203 | 56 | 39 | 35 | 8 | 1.55 |
| 1916 | 48 | 25 | 20 | 371 | 228 | 132 | 38 | 36 | 3 | 1.89 |
| 1917 | 47 | 23 | 16 | 328 | 188 | 67 | 34 | 30 | 8 | 2.30 |
| 1918 | 39 | 23 | 13 | 325 | 162 | 70 | 29 | 29 | 8 | 1.27 |
| 1919 | 39 | 20 | 14 | 290 | 147 | 51 | 29 | 27 | 7 | 1.49 |
| 1920 | 21 | 8 | 10 | 144 | 78 | 27 | 15 | 12 | 4 | 3.13 |
| 1921 | 35 | 17 | 14 | 264 | 143 | 92 | 32 | 25 | 1 | 3.51 |
| 1922 | 41 | 15 | 16 | 280 | 105 | 99 | 31 | 23 | 4 | 2.99 |
| 1923 | 43 | 17 | 12 | 262 | 130 | 69 | 35 | 18 | 3 | 3.54 |
| 1924 | 38 | 23 | 7 | 278 | 158 | 77 | 38 | 20 | 6 | 2.72 |
| 1925 | 30 | 20 | 7 | 229 | 108 | 78 | 29 | 16 | 3 | 3.07 |
| 1926 | 33 | 15 | 16 | 262 | 125 | 73 | 33 | 22 | 2 | 3.61 |
| 1927 | 18 | 5 | 6 | 108 | 48 | 26 | 15 | 7 | 1 | 5.10 |
| TOTAL | 802 | 416 | 279 | 5925 | 3508 | 1405 | 666 | 532 | 113 | 2.17 |

*For sheer numbers, not many were better than Walter Johnson. He won 416 games, more than many pitchers are permitted to start. His long reach may have been the secret behind his blazing fastball.*

# SANDY KOUFAX

*Sandy Koufax was truly a blazing comet on the baseball horizon. He didn't have the longevity enjoyed by Cy Young or Walter Johnson, but when he was at his best, no one was finer.*

*With an average of 9.27 strikeouts per nine innings, Koufax remains one of only two pitchers to average more than one strikeout per inning.*

For a period of six years, Sanford Koufax was as great a pitcher as has ever played the game. He was completely and utterly dominant.

Before 1961, the Dodgers' left-hander needed six seasons to find his control, to harness his pyrotechnic fastball and lethal curve. In 1966 his career was over, called because of arthritis. In between, Sandy Koufax combined all that raw power with superb control and set the record book on fire.

Those six seasons yielded a record 129-47 and five straight earned run average titles. Koufax threw four no-hitters in four consecutive years, something no one has yet equaled. He won the strikeout title four times and the Cy Young Award as the best pitcher in the majors three times. In particular, his 1963 and 1965 seasons were among the most brilliant in baseball history.

Koufax led the majors in strikeouts with 269 in 1961 and a year later topped the National League with an earned run average of 2.54. In 1963, it all came together. The 6-foot-2, 210-pound Brooklyn native had lost more games than he won (36-40) in his first six seasons in Brooklyn and then Los Angeles.

After going 18-13 in 1961 and 14-7 a year later, Koufax broke through with a 25-5 record in 1963. His earned run average was a formidable 1.88, he struck out 306 batters and

pitched 11 shutouts. Koufax was named the Most Valuable Player, but he deserved the award merely on the basis of his World Series performance. The Dodgers swept the New York Yankees, 4-0, chiefly because Koufax was impossible to hit. He pitched two complete game victories, allowing three earned runs and striking out 23 batters and walking only 3.

Koufax topped himself in 1965, winning 26 games and losing only 8 in 41 starts. His earned run average was 2.04, the strikeout total was a blinding 382, still a National League record. Put that in perspective by considering that the Mets' Dwight Gooden struck out 268 batters when he won the Cy Young Award in 1985. Koufax also posted a league-leading 27 complete games and eight shutouts. With the '65 World Series tied between the Dodgers and Minnesota at two-all, Koufax struck out 10 Twins and scattered four singles, leading the Dodgers to a 7-0 victory. In the seventh game he pitched his second consecutive shutout, throwing a three-hitter and recording another 10 strikeouts. In a total of 24 innings, Koufax struck out 29 batters and walked only 5. His earned run average was a scant .38.

His brilliance had its price, however. Arthritis of the left elbow forced Koufax to retire after the 1966 season, at age 31. He didn't post the career numbers of Walter Johnson or Cy Young, but for six fleeting seasons, Sandy Koufax was the pitcher of record.

*As a child on the sand lot, Sandy Koufax could bat with the best of them. As he grew, though, he found his true calling: pitching. The ball even looked lethal in his hands.*

*His motion was a thing of beauty, fluid and awe-inspiring. Sadly, Koufax's magic was short lived.*

## S T A T S

| YEAR | G | W | L | IP | SO | TBB | GS | CG | ShO | ERA |
|------|-----|-----|-----|------|------|-----|-----|-----|-----|------|
| 1955 | 12 | 2 | 2 | 42 | 30 | 28 | 5 | 2 | 2 | 3.02 |
| 1956 | 16 | 2 | 4 | 59 | 30 | 29 | 10 | 0 | 0 | 4.91 |
| 1957 | 34 | 5 | 4 | 104 | 122 | 51 | 13 | 2 | 0 | 3.88 |
| 1958 | 40 | 11 | 11 | 159 | 131 | 105 | 26 | 5 | 0 | 4.48 |
| 1959 | 35 | 8 | 6 | 153 | 173 | 92 | 23 | 6 | 1 | 4.05 |
| 1960 | 37 | 8 | 13 | 175 | 197 | 100 | 26 | 7 | 2 | 3.91 |
| 1961 | 42 | 18 | 13 | 256 | 269 | 96 | 35 | 15 | 2 | 3.52 |
| 1962 | 28 | 14 | 7 | 184 | 216 | 57 | 26 | 11 | 2 | 2.54 |
| 1963 | 40 | 25 | 5 | 311 | 306 | 58 | 40 | 20 | 11 | 1.88 |
| 1964 | 29 | 19 | 5 | 223 | 223 | 53 | 28 | 15 | 7 | 1.74 |
| 1965 | 43 | 26 | 8 | 336 | 382 | 71 | 41 | 27 | 8 | 2.04 |
| 1966 | 41 | 27 | 9 | 323 | 317 | 77 | 41 | 27 | 5 | 1.73 |
| TOTAL | 397 | 165 | 87 | 2325 | 2396 | 817 | 314 | 137 | 40 | 2.76 |

# MICKEY MANTLE

*Mickey Mantle was quick out of the batter's box for a home run hitter. An old football injury, however, forced him to take the bases slowly.*

*Mantle holds the World Series record of 18 career home runs.*

In 1931, Mickey Charles Mantle was named after Mickey Cochrane, the great American League catcher of the time. His parents must have known something.

At 19, Mantle left Spavinaw, Oklahoma to play at Joplin, Missouri, where he hit .383 with 26 home runs and 123 runs batted in. That was Class C ball, but a year later Mantle tried to make the quantum leap to the New York Yankees. He opened the season in right field with a huge burden on his back: a number 6. The Babe himself had worn number 3, Lou Gehrig had number 4, and Joe DiMaggio was still gracing center field with number 5. Obviously, much was expected from this 5-foot-11, 195-pound phenom. When his average dipped to .260, Mantle was shipped down to Kansas City for six weeks of seasoning. On return, Mantle very quietly requested number 7.

Mantle possessed that rare combination of power and speed, and he could hit the ball farther and run faster than almost anyone. He hit 536 home runs in 18 years—and he did it from both sides of the plate. No switch-hitter ever had that kind of record. Mantle, despite his riveting speed, stole only 153 bases during his career. An old football injury developed into an arrested case of osteomyelitis, a bone infection in his right leg. And so, the Yankees rarely took chances with Mantle on the base paths.

In the 1951 World Series, Mantle tore knee cartilage when he stepped on the wooden lid of a drainpipe in right-center field. Oddly enough, the ball was hit by Willie Mays and caught by DiMaggio. His legs, weak to begin with, were never quite the same. Yet Mantle accomplished some fairly amazing things. Named Most Valuable Player three times, he won it back-to-back in 1956 and 1957. In those two years, Mantle averaged .358, hit 86 home runs, and drove in 224 runs.

In 1961, when Roger Maris eclipsed Babe Ruth's record with 61 home runs, Mantle was within two of Maris as late as September 5. Typically, failing health intervened and a virus took Mantle out of the race. Still, he hit 54 homers, a total surpassed by only five men.

In 1963, a year after he won his last MVP Award, Mantle ran into the wall in Baltimore as he tried to make a catch in center field, breaking a bone in his left foot and tearing another knee cartilage. He missed most of the season and was eventually moved to first base. Historians of the game often wonder what Mantle might have accomplished if he had been healthy throughout his career.

Sometimes, however, justice does prevail. In 1974, Mantle joined his namesake in the Hall of Fame.

*Though he doesn't receive much credit for it, Mickey Mantle was a complete ballplayer. This shot, though, was staged for the camera.*

## S T A T S

| YEAR | G | AB | H | 2B | 3B | HR | TB | R | RBI | BB | AVG |
|------|------|------|------|-----|----|-----|------|------|------|------|------|
| 1951 | 96 | 341 | 91 | 11 | 5 | 13 | 151 | 61 | 65 | 43 | .267 |
| 1952 | 142 | 549 | 171 | 37 | 7 | 23 | 291 | 94 | 87 | 75 | .311 |
| 1953 | 127 | 461 | 136 | 24 | 3 | 21 | 229 | 105 | 92 | 79 | .295 |
| 1954 | 146 | 543 | 163 | 17 | 12 | 27 | 285 | 129 | 102 | 102 | .300 |
| 1955 | 147 | 517 | 158 | 25 | 11 | 37 | 316 | 121 | 99 | 113 | .306 |
| 1956 | 150 | 533 | 188 | 22 | 5 | 52 | 376 | 132 | 130 | 112 | .353 |
| 1957 | 144 | 474 | 173 | 28 | 6 | 34 | 315 | 121 | 94 | 146 | .365 |
| 1958 | 150 | 519 | 158 | 21 | 1 | 42 | 307 | 127 | 97 | 129 | .304 |
| 1959 | 144 | 541 | 154 | 23 | 4 | 31 | 278 | 104 | 75 | 94 | .285 |
| 1960 | 153 | 527 | 145 | 17 | 6 | 40 | 294 | 119 | 94 | 111 | .275 |
| 1961 | 153 | 514 | 163 | 16 | 6 | 54 | 353 | 132 | 128 | 126 | .317 |
| 1962 | 123 | 377 | 121 | 15 | 1 | 30 | 228 | 96 | 89 | 122 | .321 |
| 1963 | 65 | 172 | 54 | 8 | 0 | 15 | 107 | 40 | 35 | 40 | .314 |
| 1964 | 143 | 465 | 141 | 25 | 2 | 35 | 275 | 92 | 111 | 99 | .303 |
| 1965 | 122 | 361 | 92 | 12 | 1 | 19 | 163 | 44 | 46 | 73 | .255 |
| 1966 | 108 | 333 | 96 | 12 | 1 | 23 | 179 | 40 | 56 | 57 | .288 |
| 1967 | 144 | 440 | 108 | 17 | 0 | 22 | 191 | 63 | 55 | 107 | .245 |
| 1968 | 144 | 435 | 103 | 14 | 1 | 18 | 173 | 57 | 54 | 106 | .237 |
| **TOTAL** | **2401** | **8102** | **2415** | **344** | **72** | **536** | **4511** | **1677** | **1509** | **1734** | **.298** |

*Willie Mays had it all. Size. Speed. Power. Grace. He was the prototypical baseball player.*

# WILLIE MAYS

*Mays won 11 Gold Gloves as a center fielder for the Giants.*

Perhaps no player so excited baseball quite the way the "Say Hey Kid" did in the 1950s and 1960s. Willie Howard Mays was electric. At the plate, on the bases, in the field—especially in the field.

He tore the minor leagues up after the New York Giants signed the 19-year-old in 1950. Mays passed quickly through Trenton and Minneapolis and was called up a year later when manager Leo Durocher needed a glove for the Polo Grounds' yawning center field. Although Mays failed to hit in his first 12 at-bats, Durocher wouldn't return him to the minors. He had seen the 5-foot-10, 170-pound Mays at work in the outfield. He could chase down anything that stayed in the park and had the arm strength to make a throw from wherever his fleet feet had taken him. His speed and instincts allowed him to play closer to the infield than most center fielders, so he saved Giants pitchers numerous singles.

Eventually, the hits began to come and the Giants, too, began to find themselves. They trailed the Brooklyn Dodgers by 13½ games on August 12, 1951, but won 37 of their final 44 games and caught the Dodgers at the wire. On October 3, Bobby Thomson's home run cleared the wall in left field and another baseball legend was born. Thus, the Giants won the National League pennant and Mays' modest contribution of 20 home runs and 68 runs

batted in undoubtedly helped. The Army prevented him from making much of an impact in 1952 or 1953, but the next year Mays began a terrific run of success.

In many ways, 1954 might have been his best season; it showed the world what was possible. Through 99 games, Mays had hit 36 home runs. Even in late June he had been far ahead of Babe Ruth's record pace, but the Giants were in a pennant race with the Dodgers and Braves and Durocher needed singles in greater regularity to win. Though Mays hit only five home runs over the last two months of the season, he raised his batting average to .345, a figure that led the majors. After the Giants swept four games from Cleveland in the World Series, Mays was named the league's Most Valuable Player.

He hit 51 home runs the next season and in the following year stole 40 bases. There wasn't anything he couldn't do, as his staggering career statistics indicate: 3,283 hits, 6,066 total bases, 660 home runs, 1,903 runs batted in, 2,062 runs scored, and 338 stolen bases.

As he grew older, Mays' power showed no signs of diminishing. Between the ages of thirty and forty, Mays averaged 35 home runs per season at Candlestick Park. In 1971, at the age of forty, Mays stole 23 bases, more than he had in ten years. Say Hey.

## S T A T S

| YEAR | G | AB | H | 2B | 3B | HR | TB | R | RBI | BB | AVG |
|------|------|-------|------|-----|-----|-----|------|------|------|------|------|
| 1951 | 121 | 464 | 127 | 22 | 5 | 20 | 219 | 59 | 68 | 56 | .274 |
| 1952 | 34 | 127 | 30 | 2 | 4 | 4 | 52 | 17 | 23 | 16 | .236 |
| 1954 | 151 | 565 | 195 | 33 | 13 | 41 | 377 | 119 | 110 | 66 | .345 |
| 1955 | 152 | 580 | 185 | 18 | 13 | 51 | 382 | 123 | 127 | 79 | .319 |
| 1956 | 152 | 578 | 171 | 27 | 8 | 36 | 322 | 101 | 84 | 68 | .296 |
| 1957 | 152 | 585 | 195 | 26 | 20 | 35 | 366 | 112 | 97 | 76 | .333 |
| 1958 | 152 | 600 | 208 | 33 | 11 | 29 | 350 | 121 | 96 | 78 | .347 |
| 1959 | 151 | 575 | 180 | 43 | 5 | 34 | 335 | 125 | 104 | 65 | .313 |
| 1960 | 153 | 595 | 190 | 29 | 12 | 29 | 330 | 107 | 103 | 61 | .319 |
| 1961 | 154 | 572 | 176 | 32 | 3 | 40 | 334 | 129 | 123 | 81 | .308 |
| 1962 | 162 | 621 | 189 | 36 | 5 | 49 | 382 | 130 | 141 | 78 | .304 |
| 1963 | 157 | 596 | 187 | 32 | 7 | 38 | 347 | 115 | 103 | 66 | .314 |
| 1964 | 157 | 578 | 171 | 21 | 9 | 47 | 351 | 121 | 111 | 82 | .296 |
| 1965 | 157 | 558 | 177 | 21 | 3 | 52 | 360 | 118 | 112 | 76 | .317 |
| 1966 | 152 | 552 | 159 | 29 | 4 | 37 | 307 | 99 | 103 | 70 | .288 |
| 1967 | 141 | 486 | 128 | 22 | 2 | 22 | 220 | 83 | 70 | 51 | .263 |
| 1968 | 148 | 498 | 144 | 20 | 5 | 23 | 243 | 84 | 79 | 67 | .289 |
| 1969 | 117 | 403 | 114 | 17 | 3 | 13 | 176 | 64 | 58 | 49 | .283 |
| 1970 | 139 | 478 | 139 | 15 | 2 | 28 | 242 | 94 | 83 | 79 | .291 |
| 1971 | 136 | 417 | 113 | 24 | 5 | 18 | 201 | 82 | 61 | 112 | .271 |
| 1972 | 88 | 244 | 61 | 11 | 1 | 8 | 98 | 35 | 22 | 60 | .250 |
| 1973 | 66 | 209 | 44 | 10 | 0 | 6 | 72 | 24 | 25 | 27 | .211 |
| **TOTAL** | **2992** | **10881** | **3283** | **523** | **140** | **660** | **6066** | **2062** | **1903** | **1463** | **.302** |

*Combining incredible reflexes with the ability to twist his body like a contortionist, Willie Mays was the consummate center fielder.*

*Sometimes, the "Say Hey" kid just couldn't contain his enthusiasm. With Willie Mays, you always expected the unexpected and in most cases he delivered.*

# STAN MUSIAL

*Stan Musial was nothing if not consistent. For 13 straight seasons, he had 183 hits or more.*

*Musial appeared in 24 All-Star games.*

Like Babe Ruth, Stanley Frank Musial was once a pitcher. This was before he arrived in St. Louis, became "Stan the Man," and started hitting line drives all over the place.

He was born in Donora, Pennsylvania in 1920 and 20 years later found himself a 6-foot, 175-pound, left-handed pitcher scuffling along in Class C ball. He wasn't striking out any people and he switched to the outfield, getting the call up to the Cardinals in 1941. Musial's batting stance was a little strange; he looked like a moving corkscrew as he unleashed his body at the ball. But soon everyone knew something wonderful was at work as Musial managed 20 hits in 12 games that season. For the next 22 years (save one for the war effort in 1945), Musial moved into the starting lineup and never stopped hitting.

He wasn't a slugger, but a pure hitter who just seemed to hit doubles (725) at will. Only Tris Speaker and Pete Rose hit more and only Hank Aaron finished with more extra-base hits. The .300 batting mark is a cherished accomplishment, but Musial hit over .310 in 18 different seasons and won the National League batting title seven times.

Stamped with the hallmark of greatness, Musial withstood the test of time, producing quality in quantity. For a stretch in the 1940s, no one hit a baseball better. Musial won the Most Valuable Player Award in 1943, when he hit a league-leading .357, including 48 doubles and 20 triples. St. Louis reached the World Series but lost to the Yankees. Musial's numbers the next year were nearly as good (.347, 51 doubles, 14 triples) and the Cardinals eventually beat their cross-town rivals, the Browns, in the 1944 World Series. Musial's three hits in Game Four launched the Cardinals on a three-game winning streak.

Musial missed the 1945 season and, perhaps as a consequence, the Cardinals missed the World Series. Back the next year, he won the MVP Award a second time with a .365 average, 50 doubles and 20 triples—and St. Louis beat Boston in the 1946 World Series. In 1948, Musial hit .376, slugged .702 and put together a routine 46 doubles and 18 triples. He was named MVP again, for the third time in five seasons.

In 1952, Musial made his only major league appearance on the mound. He didn't allow a hit, nor did he get anyone out. That's why they made him a hitter.

# BROOKS ROBINSON

*Brooks Robinson successfully handled 8,902 of 9,165 chances at third base, for a major league fielding percentage record of .971.*

I t isn't often that a player makes a lasting impact on baseball. It is even rarer when he does it without a bat or a ball. Brooks Calbert Robinson was a glove man, the best third baseman the game has ever seen. He made defense fashionable in the modern era by winning 16 consecutive Gold Glove Awards as his position's best fielder.

Robinson played in more games (2,687), handled more chances (9,165), produced more assists (6,205), and was involved in more double plays (618) than any other third baseman. His career batting average of .267 is almost a moot point.

When he emerged from Little Rock, Arkansas in 1955, Robinson left in his wake a number of critics who claimed the 6-foot-1, 180-pounder wasn't fast enough to make the majors. Yet the Baltimore Orioles liked what they saw and called him up at the age of 18. Robinson produced only two hits in 22 at-bats and spent the next four years bounding between Baltimore and places like San Antonio and Vancouver. When he returned from the minor leagues for the last time on July 9, 1959, Robinson played in 97 percent of the Orioles' games over the next sixteen years.

And, contrary to perceptions, Robinson had a serviceable bat. The right-hander hit .303 in 1962 and .317 two years later, knocked in 100 runs or more twice, and hit 20 or more home runs six different times. Robinson's 268 career home runs were a record for American League third basemen at one time. His career League Championship Series is .348, which says something about his ability to deliver under duress. In 1964, he was the league's MVP.

It is the memory of his glove, though, that people cherish. In 1970, he carried the Orioles to a five-game World Series victory over the Cincinnati Reds. Baltimore won the first three games, its 17th in a row. In that third game, Robinson destroyed the spirit of the Reds' right-handed power hitters, reaching two sure hits down the line and pounding a two-run double. When Baltimore had prevailed, Robinson was named Most Valuable Player on the basis of his magnificent fielding performance, not to mention a .429 batting average, two home runs, and six runs batted in.

The end came in 1977. Robinson was 40 years old, battling Cleveland reliever Dave LaRoche. He was pinch-hitting for Larry Harlow in a tenth-inning game the Orioles trailed

5-3. With two men on base, he ran the count to three-and-two, fouled off several pitches, then hit the ball over the fence in left field. It was his last home run and one of baseball's more emotional moments.

## S T A T S

| YEAR | G | AB | H | 2B | 3B | HR | TB | R | RBI | BB | AVG |
|---|---|---|---|---|---|---|---|---|---|---|---|
| 1955 | 6 | 22 | 2 | 0 | 0 | 0 | 2 | 0 | 1 | 0 | .091 |
| 1956 | 15 | 44 | 10 | 4 | 0 | 1 | 17 | 5 | 1 | 1 | .227 |
| 1957 | 50 | 117 | 28 | 6 | 1 | 2 | 42 | 13 | 14 | 7 | .239 |
| 1958 | 145 | 463 | 110 | 16 | 3 | 3 | 141 | 31 | 32 | 31 | .238 |
| 1959 | 88 | 313 | 89 | 15 | 2 | 4 | 120 | 29 | 24 | 17 | .284 |
| 1960 | 152 | 595 | 175 | 27 | 9 | 14 | 262 | 74 | 88 | 35 | .294 |
| 1961 | 163 | 668 | 192 | 38 | 7 | 7 | 265 | 89 | 61 | 47 | .287 |
| 1962 | 162 | 634 | 192 | 29 | 9 | 23 | 308 | 77 | 86 | 42 | .303 |
| 1963 | 161 | 589 | 148 | 26 | 4 | 11 | 215 | 67 | 67 | 46 | .251 |
| 1964 | 163 | 612 | 194 | 35 | 3 | 28 | 319 | 82 | 118 | 51 | .317 |
| 1965 | 144 | 559 | 166 | 25 | 2 | 18 | 249 | 81 | 80 | 47 | .297 |
| 1966 | 157 | 620 | 167 | 35 | 2 | 23 | 275 | 91 | 100 | 56 | .269 |
| 1967 | 158 | 610 | 164 | 25 | 5 | 22 | 265 | 88 | 77 | 54 | .269 |
| 1968 | 162 | 608 | 154 | 36 | 6 | 17 | 253 | 65 | 75 | 44 | .253 |
| 1969 | 156 | 598 | 140 | 21 | 3 | 23 | 236 | 73 | 84 | 56 | .234 |
| 1970 | 158 | 608 | 168 | 31 | 4 | 18 | 261 | 84 | 94 | 53 | .276 |
| 1971 | 156 | 589 | 160 | 21 | 1 | 20 | 243 | 67 | 92 | 63 | .272 |
| 1972 | 153 | 556 | 139 | 23 | 2 | 8 | 190 | 48 | 64 | 43 | .250 |
| 1973 | 155 | 549 | 141 | 17 | 2 | 9 | 189 | 53 | 72 | 55 | .257 |
| 1974 | 153 | 553 | 159 | 27 | 0 | 7 | 207 | 46 | 59 | 56 | .288 |
| 1975 | 144 | 482 | 97 | 15 | 1 | 6 | 132 | 50 | 53 | 44 | .201 |
| 1976 | 71 | 218 | 46 | 8 | 2 | 3 | 67 | 16 | 11 | 8 | .211 |
| 1977 | 24 | 47 | 7 | 2 | 0 | 1 | 12 | 3 | 4 | 4 | .149 |
| TOTAL | 2896 | 10654 | 2848 | 482 | 68 | 268 | 4270 | 1232 | 1357 | 860 | .267 |

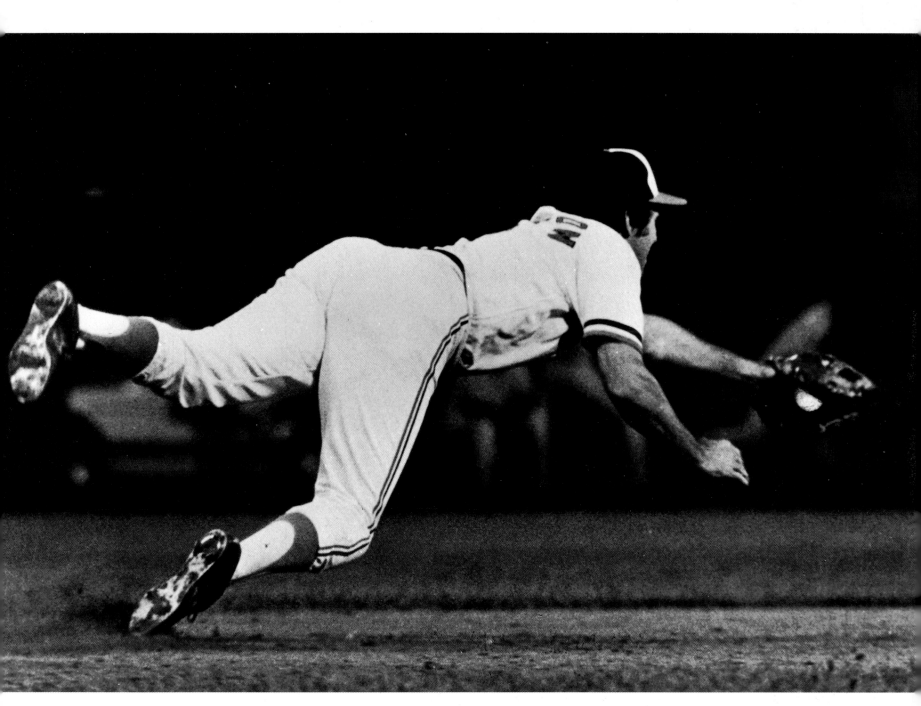

*Out of the frying pan and into the hole between third and shortstop—that was Brooks Robinson's forte.*

# PETE ROSE

*For nine straight seasons, from 1965 to 1973, Rose batted better than .300.*

H e ran when others walked.

Critics said it wasn't necessary, not to mention downright arrogant, but this was merely "Charlie Hustle's" way of wearing his aggressive heart on his sleeve. And so, Peter Edward Rose ran into the record books with elbows and dust flying everywhere.

Rose, a solid 5-foot-11, 200-pound switch-hitter, made hitting singles respectable in a sport where home runs are very much the main attraction. When he was finished, Rose had established searing career standards for future generations to contemplate: most hits (4,256); games played (3,562); plate appearances (14,053); singles (3,215); and seasons with 200 or more hits (10).

Rose did everything with a little extra gusto, which is why he played until the age of 45. In fact, 1986 was the first season in 24 that Rose did not play in 100 games, because he happened to be managing his Cincinnati Reds at the time.

There was a down side to all that hustling, however. Rose, as it turned out, was a heavy sports gambler. In the spring of 1989, he was suspended from baseball when it was alleged that he had bet on his own Cincinnati Reds. Rose went to jail for a spell and was formally removed from the list of players eligible for the Hall of Fame.

On the field, Rose believed that giving the most of yourself was the only way to approach a task. Whether it was daring baserunning or playing the outfield, Rose, well, hustled. Invari-

ably, he took the extra base or caught the ball that looked to be out of reach. People are surprised to hear that based on Rose's lifetime fielding percentage of .991, he is certifiably one of the best outfielders ever.

This, from the young second baseman who at age 19 committed a league-leading 36 errors for Geneva of the New York–Pennsylvania League in 1960. Rose weathered that storm, however, and was promoted to the Florida State League's Tampa franchise. There, he led the league with 160 hits in 130 games, including 30 triples. Another year in Macon, Georgia, prepared him for spring training in 1963.

While the rest of the players were going through the motions, Rose was hurtling all over the field. It was Mickey Mantle who commented one day, "Look at Charlie Hustle." He didn't mean it kindly, but Rose took it as a compliment. He made the Reds team and was named the National League's Rookie of the Year for hitting .273. Through the next 16 remarkable seasons, Rose hit .300 or better for 14 of those years and produced more than 200 hits in 10 of them.

And on September 11, 1985, Rose found himself at Cincinnati's Riverfront Stadium staring out at San Diego's Eric Show. The 2-1 slider was inside and low, but Rose hacked at it and the ball bounced in front of left fielder Carmelo Martinez. It was Rose's 4,192 career base hit and pushed him one past the great Ty Cobb. And he ran all the way to first base.

*Efficiency was Pete Rose's greatest talent. He took his rather common resources and produced an uncommon body of baseball work.*

## S T A T S

| YEAR | G | AB | H | 2B | 3B | HR | TB | R | RBI | BB | AVG |
|------|------|-------|------|-----|-----|-----|------|------|------|------|------|
| 1963 | 157 | 623 | 170 | 25 | 9 | 6 | 231 | 101 | 41 | 55 | .273 |
| 1964 | 136 | 516 | 139 | 13 | 2 | 4 | 168 | 64 | 34 | 36 | .269 |
| 1965 | 162 | 670 | 209 | 35 | 11 | 11 | 299 | 117 | 81 | 69 | .312 |
| 1966 | 156 | 654 | 205 | 38 | 5 | 16 | 301 | 97 | 70 | 37 | .313 |
| 1967 | 148 | 585 | 176 | 32 | 8 | 12 | 260 | 86 | 76 | 56 | .301 |
| 1968 | 149 | 626 | 210 | 42 | 6 | 10 | 294 | 94 | 49 | 56 | .335 |
| 1969 | 156 | 627 | 218 | 33 | 11 | 16 | 321 | 120 | 82 | 88 | .348 |
| 1970 | 159 | 649 | 205 | 37 | 9 | 15 | 305 | 120 | 52 | 73 | .316 |
| 1971 | 160 | 632 | 192 | 27 | 4 | 13 | 266 | 86 | 44 | 68 | .304 |
| 1972 | 154 | 645 | 198 | 31 | 11 | 6 | 269 | 107 | 57 | 73 | .307 |
| 1973 | 160 | 680 | 230 | 36 | 8 | 5 | 297 | 115 | 64 | 65 | .338 |
| 1974 | 163 | 652 | 185 | 45 | 7 | 3 | 253 | 110 | 51 | 106 | .284 |
| 1975 | 162 | 662 | 210 | 47 | 4 | 7 | 286 | 112 | 74 | 89 | .317 |
| 1976 | 162 | 665 | 215 | 42 | 6 | 10 | 299 | 130 | 63 | 86 | .323 |
| 1977 | 162 | 655 | 204 | 38 | 7 | 9 | 283 | 95 | 64 | 66 | .311 |
| 1978 | 159 | 655 | 198 | 51 | 3 | 7 | 276 | 103 | 52 | 62 | .302 |
| 1979 | 163 | 628 | 208 | 40 | 5 | 4 | 270 | 90 | 59 | 95 | .331 |
| 1980 | 162 | 655 | 185 | 42 | 1 | 1 | 232 | 95 | 64 | 66 | .282 |
| 1981 | 107 | 431 | 140 | 18 | 5 | 0 | 168 | 73 | 33 | 46 | .325 |
| 1982 | 162 | 634 | 172 | 25 | 4 | 3 | 214 | 80 | 54 | 66 | .271 |
| 1983 | 151 | 493 | 121 | 14 | 3 | 0 | 141 | 52 | 45 | 52 | .245 |
| 1984 | 121 | 374 | 107 | 15 | 2 | 0 | 126 | 43 | 34 | 40 | .286 |
| 1985 | 119 | 405 | 107 | 12 | 2 | 2 | 129 | 60 | 46 | 86 | .264 |
| 1986 | 72 | 237 | 52 | 8 | 2 | 0 | 64 | 15 | 25 | 30 | .219 |
| TOTAL | 3562 | 14053 | 4256 | 746 | 135 | 160 | 5752 | 2165 | 1314 | 1566 | .303 |

*Always, Pete Rose studied the game, the count, the situation. It was this curiosity which led to his ascension to the Cincinnati Reds' manager.*

# BABE RUTH

*Ruth has baseball's best home run/at-bats ratio, with a homer for every 11.76 at-bats. Hank Aaron, who broke his 714-homer mark, has a ratio of 16.38.*

Rarely does one man come to personify an entire sport. It happened in baseball, though, in the form of George Herman Ruth, The Sultan of Swat, The Bambino. The Babe.

Ruth was born in Baltimore in 1895. At 19, just out of St. Mary's Industrial Home for Boys in Baltimore, he was purchased from the bankrupt Orioles by the Red Sox for $2,900. Ruth was hardly a heavy hitter at the time. His first season in the big leagues brought him exactly 10 at-bats (he got two hits, including a double), because Babe was a pitcher. The 6-foot-2, 215-pound left-hander was a good one, too. The next year, Ruth led the American League with 18 victories and only 8 losses—he also was permitted to bat 92 times, resulting in 29 hits, four of them home runs. Manager Rough Carrigan quickly discovered Ruth's ability with the bat and used him frequently as a left-handed pinch-hitter.

While the Red Sox were in the process of winning three World Series in four years, Ruth continued to flower as a hitter. In fact, when Boston capped its flurry with a victory over Chicago in six games, it was Ruth's last year of substance on the mound. Two World Series wins paled by comparison to the .300 average he fashioned in 317 at-bats over the regular season. His 11 home runs led the league. In 1919, his last year with the Red Sox, Ruth was

9-5 on the mound and batted .322 at the plate. He also hit 29 home runs to lead the league.

That was enough to set the New York Yankees salivating. When Boston owner Harry Frazee found himself in a financial bind, he shipped Ruth to New York in exchange for $125,000 in cash and a $300,000 loan. Ruth pitched in only five more games the rest of his career and, not surprisingly, won all of them.

Responding immediately to his new environment, Ruth hit 54 homers in 1920. He added 59 more the next season, scored 177 runs and drove in 171. Ruth walked 144 times that year, something he was to do better than anyone in baseball. Such was his eye at the plate and the respect he commanded.

Mere numbers fail to adequately describe the impact Ruth had on baseball. He is still the all-time leader in slugging average (.690), home run percentage (8.5), and bases on balls (2,056). When Hank Aaron passed Ruth's record 714 home runs in 1974, the sports world watched, not quite sure how to feel. He remains the number two man, behind Aaron, in home runs and runs batted in. And only Ty Cobb crossed the plate more times than Ruth.

It might have happened differently. Ruth might have become one of the best pitchers in history as his 94-46 lifetime record suggests. He settled for being the best slugger.

*Here he is, the stuff of legends. Babe Ruth is a rarity—he lived up to all those amazing stories told about him.*

*Even during his career, Babe Ruth transcended the game. And, after he retired, his fame grew even greater.*

## S T A T S

| YEAR | G | AB | H | 2B | 3B | HR | TB | R | RBI | BB | AVG |
|------|------|------|------|-----|-----|-----|------|------|------|------|------|
| 1914 | 5 | 10 | 2 | 1 | 0 | 0 | 3 | 1 | 0 | 0 | .200 |
| 1915 | 42 | 92 | 29 | 10 | 1 | 4 | 53 | 16 | 20 | 9 | .315 |
| 1916 | 67 | 136 | 37 | 5 | 3 | 3 | 57 | 18 | 16 | 10 | .272 |
| 1917 | 52 | 123 | 40 | 6 | 3 | 2 | 58 | 14 | 10 | 12 | .325 |
| 1918 | 95 | 317 | 95 | 26 | 11 | 11 | 176 | 50 | 64 | 57 | .300 |
| 1919 | 130 | 432 | 139 | 34 | 12 | 29 | 284 | 103 | 112 | 101 | .322 |
| 1920 | 142 | 458 | 172 | 36 | 9 | 54 | 388 | 158 | 137 | 148 | .376 |
| 1921 | 152 | 540 | 204 | 44 | 16 | 59 | 457 | 177 | 171 | 144 | .378 |
| 1922 | 110 | 406 | 128 | 24 | 8 | 35 | 273 | 94 | 99 | 84 | .315 |
| 1923 | 152 | 522 | 205 | 45 | 13 | 41 | 399 | 151 | 131 | 170 | .393 |
| 1924 | 153 | 529 | 200 | 39 | 7 | 46 | 391 | 143 | 121 | 142 | .378 |
| 1925 | 98 | 359 | 104 | 12 | 2 | 25 | 195 | 61 | 66 | 59 | .290 |
| 1926 | 152 | 495 | 184 | 30 | 5 | 47 | 365 | 139 | 145 | 144 | .372 |
| 1927 | 151 | 540 | 192 | 29 | 8 | 60 | 417 | 158 | 164 | 138 | .356 |
| 1928 | 154 | 536 | 173 | 29 | 8 | 54 | 380 | 163 | 142 | 135 | .323 |
| 1929 | 135 | 499 | 172 | 26 | 6 | 46 | 348 | 121 | 154 | 72 | .345 |
| 1930 | 145 | 518 | 186 | 28 | 9 | 49 | 379 | 150 | 153 | 136 | .359 |
| 1931 | 145 | 534 | 199 | 31 | 3 | 46 | 374 | 149 | 163 | 128 | .373 |
| 1932 | 133 | 457 | 156 | 13 | 5 | 41 | 302 | 120 | 137 | 130 | .341 |
| 1933 | 137 | 459 | 138 | 21 | 3 | 34 | 267 | 97 | 103 | 114 | .301 |
| 1934 | 125 | 365 | 105 | 17 | 4 | 22 | 196 | 78 | 84 | 103 | .288 |
| 1935 | 28 | 72 | 13 | 0 | 0 | 6 | 31 | 13 | 12 | 20 | .181 |
| TOTAL | 2503 | 8399 | 2873 | 506 | 136 | 714 | 5793 | 2174 | 2204 | 2056 | .342 |

# NOLAN RYAN

*Ryan struck out 19 batters in a game four different times.*

Smoke, pure smoke. That is the essence of Lynn Nolan Ryan. Nobody did it better. No one ever threw faster than Ryan. His fastball was clocked at 100.8 miles an hour during one game in 1974, but the sight of opposing batters leaving the batter's box in a daze suggests Ryan is faster still.

For sheer firepower, the 6-foot-2, 200-pound right-hander is baseball's best. His consistency is nothing short of amazing. Through 1991, at the age of 45, Ryan had struck out 5,511 batters, the all-time record. When he was throwing strikes—his total of 2,686 bases on balls is also a record—Ryan was just about impossible to hit.

The numbers back him up. On September 26, 1981, Ryan became the first man in history to throw five no-hitters. Nine years later, on June 11, 1990, Ryan no-hit Oakland for his sixth gem. Impossibly, on May 1, 1991, it happened again. At the age of 44, Ryan threw his seventh no-hitter, a 3-0 Texas Ranger victory over Toronto. He struck out 16 batters in that game. The near-misses are just as impressive. Ryan has thrown a total of 12 one-hitters.

He was born in Refugio, Texas, and 18 years later in 1965, Ryan was an eighth-round draft choice of the New York Mets. In 1966, Ryan led the Western Carolina League with 272 strikeouts and a 17-2 record. From that single-A club, he made the jump all the way to the majors in one season's time. Ryan spent four full seasons with the Amazin' Mets, including 1969's impossible championship season. In 1971, he was traded to the California Angels along with three other players in exchange for Jim Fregosi. What followed was similarly amazin'.

In his eight years with the Angels, Ryan led the American League seven times in strikeouts. He averaged 302 Ks a year over that time. Of course, Ryan also was leading the league in bases on balls in six of those eight years, which is one reason his overall record is 314-278.

Still, Ryan's talent is immense; of his 314 career victories, 61 were shutouts. And not only had he fanned 5,511 batters, but he had the major league's best strikeout ratio. For every nine innings he pitched, Ryan struck out more than nine batters. Sandy Koufax was the only other pitcher with more than 1,500 innings pitched who could claim that distinction.

Ryan's longevity is beginning to border on the ridiculous. In 1991, at the age of 44, 13 seasons after the Angels allowed him to become a free agent because they believed he was too old, Ryan produced a sparkling 12-6 record. His earned run average of 2.91 was fifth in the American league, and his 203 strikeouts (in 173 innings) placed him third in the league. Now, that's amazin'.

### S T A T S

| YEAR | G | W | L | IP | SO | TBB | GS | CG | ShO | ERA |
|------|------|------|------|------|------|------|------|------|------|------|
| 1966 | 2 | 0 | 1 | 3 | 6 | 3 | 1 | 0 | 0 | 15.00 |
| 1968 | 21 | 6 | 9 | 134 | 133 | 75 | 18 | 3 | 0 | 3.09 |
| 1969 | 25 | 6 | 3 | 89 | 92 | 53 | 10 | 2 | 0 | 3.53 |
| 1970 | 27 | 7 | 11 | 132 | 125 | 97 | 19 | 5 | 2 | 3.41 |
| 1971 | 30 | 10 | 14 | 152 | 137 | 116 | 26 | 3 | 0 | 3.97 |
| 1972 | 39 | 19 | 16 | 284 | 329 | 157 | 39 | 20 | 9 | 2.28 |
| 1973 | 41 | 21 | 16 | 326 | 383 | 162 | 39 | 26 | 4 | 2.87 |
| 1974 | 42 | 22 | 16 | 333 | 367 | 202 | 41 | 26 | 3 | 2.89 |
| 1975 | 28 | 14 | 12 | 198 | 186 | 132 | 28 | 10 | 5 | 3.45 |
| 1976 | 39 | 17 | 18 | 284 | 327 | 183 | 39 | 21 | 7 | 3.36 |
| 1977 | 37 | 19 | 16 | 299 | 341 | 204 | 37 | 22 | 4 | 2.77 |
| 1978 | 31 | 10 | 13 | 235 | 260 | 148 | 31 | 14 | 3 | 2.71 |
| 1979 | 34 | 16 | 14 | 223 | 223 | 114 | 34 | 17 | 5 | 3.59 |
| 1980 | 35 | 11 | 10 | 234 | 200 | 98 | 35 | 4 | 2 | 3.35 |
| 1981 | 21 | 11 | 5 | 149 | 140 | 68 | 21 | 5 | 3 | 1.69 |
| 1982 | 35 | 16 | 12 | 250 | 245 | 109 | 35 | 10 | 3 | 3.16 |
| 1983 | 29 | 14 | 9 | 196 | 183 | 101 | 29 | 5 | 2 | 2.98 |
| 1984 | 30 | 12 | 11 | 184 | 197 | 69 | 30 | 5 | 2 | 3.04 |
| 1985 | 35 | 10 | 12 | 232 | 209 | 95 | 35 | 4 | 0 | 3.80 |
| 1986 | 30 | 12 | 8 | 178 | 194 | 82 | 30 | 1 | 0 | 3.34 |
| 1987 | 34 | 8 | 18 | 212 | 270 | 87 | 34 | 0 | 0 | 2.76 |
| 1988 | 33 | 12 | 11 | 220 | 228 | 87 | 33 | 4 | 1 | 3.52 |
| 1989 | 32 | 16 | 10 | 239 | 301 | 98 | 32 | 6 | 2 | 3.20 |
| 1990 | 30 | 13 | 9 | 204 | 232 | 74 | 30 | 8 | 2 | 3.44 |
| 1991 | 27 | 12 | 6 | 173 | 203 | 72 | 27 | 2 | 2 | 2.91 |
| TOTAL | 767 | 314 | 278 | 5163 | 5511 | 2686 | 733 | 220 | 61 | 3.15 |

*Even at the age of 40, Nolan Ryan had an extremely live arm. His fastball struck panic in the hearts of hitters everywhere.*

# MIKE SCHMIDT

*With his bat (35 homers or more for 12 seasons) or his glove (10 Gold Gloves), Mike Schmidt could beat you.*

---

*Schmidt has led the National League in home runs eight different times.*

---

When they vote Michael Jack Schmidt into baseball's Hall of Fame (he's eligible in 1994), he will be considered one of the game's all-time greats. He finished his career in 1989 with 548 home runs, seventh on the all-time list. Consider the first six: Hank Aaron, Babe Ruth, Willie Mays, Frank Robinson, Harmon Killebrew, and Reggie Jackson.

In an 18-year career, Schmidt had 11 seasons with 35 homers or more, a figure surpassed only by Ruth and Aaron, and they played 22 and 23 seasons, respectively. Schmidt also had one of the best home-runs-to-at-bats ratios (1 for every 15.2 at-bats) in major-league history.

The 6-foot-2, 203-pound third baseman was named the National League's Most Valuable Player three times, including 1980 and 1981. Only Stan Musial and Roy Campanella equaled that feat. Schmidt was selected to play in 10 All-Star games and won 10 Gold Gloves for fielding excellence, another league record.

He was born in Dayton, Ohio, and eventually earned a degree in business administration from Ohio University in 1971. The Philadelphia Phillies assigned him to their Reading club, where Schmidt batted .211 and hit 8 home runs in 74 games. At Eugene the next year, Schmidt hiked his average to .291 (despite 145 strikeouts) and was called up by the Phillies late in the season. He hit one homer in 34 at-bats, a rough start that was underlined by his first full season in 1973. Schmidt batted .196 and hit 18 home runs in 132 games. For the next 16 seasons, however, Schmidt hit at least 30 home runs in all but three.

From 1974 to 1977, Schmidt averaged 38 home runs and 105 runs batted in. He led the National League in strikeouts three times over that span, but that is the traditional price sluggers pay for their awesome power. In 1976, Schmidt hit four consecutive homers against the Chicago Cubs at Wrigley Field. In fact, through 1986, he had 39 two-homer games.

In 1980, Schmidt led the league with a career-high 48 home runs and 121 runs batted in. In the World Series against the Kansas City Royals, he was named Most Valuable Player on the strength of his .381 batting average, 2 home runs, and 7 runs batted in. In 1986, at the age of 37, Schmidt again led the league in home runs (37) and runs batted in (119). In 1987, his last effective season, Schmidt cranked out 35 home runs and 113 runs batted in.

## S T A T S

| YEAR | G | AB | H | 2B | 3B | HR | TB | R | RBI | BB | AVG |
|------|------|------|------|-----|----|-----|------|------|------|------|------|
| 1972 | 13 | 34 | 7 | 0 | 0 | 1 | 10 | 2 | 3 | 5 | .206 |
| 1973 | 132 | 367 | 72 | 11 | 0 | 18 | 137 | 43 | 52 | 62 | .196 |
| 1974 | 162 | 568 | 160 | 28 | 7 | 36 | 310 | 108 | 116 | 106 | .282 |
| 1975 | 158 | 562 | 140 | 34 | 3 | 38 | 294 | 93 | 95 | 101 | .249 |
| 1976 | 160 | 584 | 153 | 31 | 4 | 38 | 306 | 112 | 107 | 100 | .262 |
| 1977 | 154 | 544 | 149 | 27 | 11 | 38 | 312 | 114 | 101 | 104 | .274 |
| 1978 | 145 | 513 | 129 | 27 | 2 | 21 | 223 | 93 | 78 | 91 | .251 |
| 1979 | 160 | 541 | 137 | 25 | 4 | 45 | 305 | 109 | 114 | 120 | .253 |
| 1980 | 150 | 548 | 157 | 25 | 8 | 48 | 342 | 104 | 121 | 89 | .286 |
| 1981 | 102 | 354 | 112 | 19 | 2 | 31 | 228 | 78 | 91 | 73 | .316 |
| 1982 | 148 | 514 | 144 | 26 | 3 | 35 | 281 | 108 | 87 | 107 | .280 |
| 1983 | 154 | 534 | 136 | 16 | 4 | 40 | 280 | 104 | 109 | 128 | .255 |
| 1984 | 151 | 528 | 146 | 23 | 3 | 36 | 283 | 93 | 106 | 92 | .277 |
| 1985 | 158 | 549 | 152 | 31 | 5 | 33 | 292 | 89 | 93 | 87 | .277 |
| 1986 | 160 | 552 | 160 | 29 | 1 | 37 | 302 | 97 | 119 | 89 | .290 |
| 1987 | 147 | 522 | 153 | 28 | 0 | 35 | 286 | 88 | 113 | 83 | .293 |
| 1988 | 108 | 390 | 97 | 21 | 2 | 12 | 158 | 52 | 62 | 49 | .249 |
| 1989 | 42 | 148 | 30 | 7 | 0 | 6 | 55 | 19 | 28 | 21 | .203 |
| **TOTAL** | **2404** | **8352** | **2234** | **408** | **59** | **548** | **4404** | **1506** | **1595** | **1507** | **.267** |

*When people remember the 1969 Mets,
they think of Tom Terrific on the mound
and the wonders he created.*

# TOM SEAVER

*For nine consecutive seasons, from 1968 to 1976, Seaver struck out more than 200 batters per year, a major-league record.*

When the Atlanta Braves tried to sign Tom Seaver out of Fresno City College in 1965, then-Commissioner William Eckert nullified the contract because a reported $40,000 signing bonus violated the school's rules. As a result, four teams put their names in a hat for Seaver and the pitiful New York Mets, who had averaged 113 losses for three seasons, finally won something: a pitcher. It wasn't long before they won the whole thing.

When George Thomas Seaver entered professional baseball he wasn't yet known as "Tom Terrific," but the 6-foot, 210-pound right-hander clearly was something special. He spent the 1966 season in Jacksonville, then stepped into the breach. Though the Mets lost 101 games in 1967, Seaver somehow managed 16 victories and was named the National League's Rookie of the Year. In the process, Seaver rewrote the Mets' pitching record book. He improved in virtually every category the next year, compiling a 16-12 record that only began to suggest the things to come.

The Mets, who were 73-89 in 1968, stunned the baseball world with a 100-62 record in 1969. Amazin' wasn't the word for it. They trailed the Chicago Cubs at one time by 9½ games, but rode Seaver's arm to the Eastern Division title. In early September with the season on the line, Seaver threw a one-hitter at the Cubs—Jimmy Qualls' ninth-inning single ruined a perfect game. The Mets won going away, by eight games, and Seaver's pitching was the reason: he finished with a 25-7 record, 208 strikeouts, and an earned run average of 2.21. The World Series victory over Baltimore was almost anti-climactic.

In 1970, Seaver led the league with 283 strikeouts and duplicated the feat five times in seven years. In all, he had ten seasons with 200 or more strikeouts. On April 22, 1970, Seaver struck out 19 San Diego Padres, including the last 10 in a row, setting a major-league record. When he left the National League in 1984, Seaver owned the league record for lowest career earned run average (2.73) for a 200-game winner and the most strikeouts (3,272) by a right-handed pitcher.

His consistency was frightening. Seaver produced winning records in his first 15 consecutive seasons and won 311 games when he finished up with Boston in 1986. A strikeout total of 3,640 placed him third on the all-time list behind Nolan Ryan and Steve Carlton.

And in his last official season, 1986, Seaver wanted to play for a team within a few hours of his Connecticut home. It was a right he was due, for he had achieved everything baseball had to offer. Seaver eventually chose Boston and helped the Red Sox to the World Series 20 years after the Mets had plucked their fortunes from a fedora.

Then in 1987, the Mets appealed to their former ace when injuries decimated the pitching staff. Seaver signed a contract and agreed to try to pitch his way back into form. It never happened. "Baseball is a young man's game," said Seaver. "And I didn't feel like I could contribute the way I wanted to."

It was vintage Seaver, a candid appraisal of the facts in hand. His contributions are now immortalized in Cooperstown, New York.

## S T A T S

| YEAR | G | W | L | IP | SO | TBB | GS | CG | ShO | ERA |
|------|-----|-----|-----|------|------|------|-----|-----|-----|------|
| 1967 | 35 | 16 | 13 | 251 | 170 | 78 | 34 | 18 | 2 | 2.76 |
| 1968 | 36 | 16 | 12 | 278 | 205 | 48 | 35 | 14 | 5 | 2.20 |
| 1969 | 36 | 25 | 7 | 273 | 208 | 82 | 35 | 18 | 5 | 2.21 |
| 1970 | 37 | 18 | 12 | 291 | 283 | 83 | 36 | 19 | 2 | 2.81 |
| 1971 | 36 | 20 | 10 | 286 | 289 | 61 | 35 | 21 | 4 | 1.76 |
| 1972 | 35 | 21 | 12 | 262 | 249 | 77 | 35 | 13 | 3 | 2.92 |
| 1973 | 36 | 19 | 10 | 290 | 251 | 64 | 36 | 18 | 3 | 2.08 |
| 1974 | 32 | 11 | 11 | 236 | 201 | 75 | 32 | 12 | 5 | 3.20 |
| 1975 | 36 | 22 | 9 | 280 | 243 | 88 | 36 | 15 | 5 | 2.38 |
| 1976 | 35 | 14 | 11 | 271 | 235 | 77 | 34 | 13 | 5 | 2.59 |
| 1977 | 33 | 21 | 6 | 261 | 196 | 66 | 33 | 19 | 7 | 2.59 |
| 1978 | 36 | 16 | 14 | 260 | 226 | 89 | 36 | 8 | 1 | 2.87 |
| 1979 | 32 | 16 | 6 | 215 | 131 | 61 | 32 | 9 | 5 | 3.14 |
| 1980 | 26 | 10 | 8 | 168 | 101 | 59 | 26 | 5 | 1 | 3.64 |
| 1981 | 23 | 14 | 2 | 166 | 87 | 66 | 23 | 6 | 1 | 2.55 |
| 1982 | 21 | 5 | 13 | 111 | 62 | 44 | 21 | 0 | 0 | 5.50 |
| 1983 | 34 | 9 | 14 | 231 | 135 | 86 | 34 | 5 | 2 | 3.55 |
| 1984 | 34 | 15 | 11 | 237 | 131 | 61 | 33 | 10 | 4 | 3.95 |
| 1985 | 35 | 16 | 11 | 240 | 134 | 69 | 33 | 6 | 1 | 3.17 |
| 1986 | 28 | 7 | 13 | 176 | 103 | 56 | 28 | 2 | 0 | 4.03 |
| **TOTAL** | **656** | **311** | **205** | **4783** | **3640** | **1390** | **647** | **231** | **61** | **2.86** |

# HONUS WAGNER

*Wagner hit well over .300 in each of his first 17 seasons in the major leagues.*

Just who is baseball's greatest player? Even with a roster that included Babe Ruth and Ty Cobb, many would choose "The Flying Dutchman," John Honus Wagner. John McGraw, the legendary manager of the New York Giants for thirty years, insisted "Wagner was the best." Go ahead and argue with that.

There can be no argument that Honus Wagner was the quintessential "complete" player. Think of a prototypical shortstop today and one visualizes an Ozzie Smith, a graceful, spider-like player with a glove as big as his strike zone. Wagner was 5-foot-11, and a substantial 200 pounds. He did not look like a shortstop; in fact, he bounced around the outfield until manager Fred Clarke moved him to shortstop in 1901. But Wagner had huge hands—reaching for some tobacco one day at first base, his hand bccamc stuck in his back pocket and eventually had to be cut free. Wagner's long arms gave him an uncommon range; he seemed to get to everything. Wagner had a strong arm and like most good shortstops, could throw from any position on the field. It was the same way with batting— he could hit any one at any time. To be sure, this was not a typical shortstop.

Wagner was a right-hander who, curiously, gripped the bat in the same fashion as Cobb, with his hands held a few inches apart. Just as Cobb terrorized the American League, so Wagner played above everybody in the National League, with the Pittsburgh Pirates for the last 18 years of his career. He broke in with Louisville in 1897, then moved to Pittsburgh with the franchise in 1900.

Wagner won eight National League batting titles, including four in a row, from 1906 to 1909. He averaged .346 over that period and helped defeat Cobb and the Detroit Tigers in the World Series of 1909 in the first season at Forbes Field. His consistent production, in terms of runs scored and batted in, was phenomenal. In a 21-year career, Wagner averaged 83 runs and 82 RBIs per year. His career average was .329. He also finished with 720 stolen bases and led the league five times in that category.

Quite simply, Wagner got the most from his talent. He preyed on mistakes by opposing pitchers. Like Joe Medwick, he was a classic "bad ball" hitter. The results, more often than not, were undeniably good.

*Over a career that spanned 21 seasons, Honus Wagner averaged .329 at the plate and threw some pretty mean leather at shortstop.*

## S T A T S

| YEAR | G | AB | H | 2B | 3B | HR | TB | R | RBI | BB | AVG |
|------|------|-------|------|-----|-----|-----|------|------|------|-----|------|
| 1897 | 61 | 241 | 83 | 17 | 4 | 2 | 114 | 38 | 39 | 15 | .344 |
| 1898 | 151 | 591 | 180 | 31 | 4 | 10 | 249 | 80 | 105 | 31 | .305 |
| 1899 | 147 | 571 | 197 | 47 | 13 | 7 | 291 | 102 | 113 | 40 | .345 |
| 1900 | 135 | 528 | 201 | 45 | 22 | 4 | 302 | 107 | 100 | 41 | .381 |
| 1901 | 141 | 556 | 196 | 39 | 10 | 6 | 273 | 100 | 126 | 53 | .353 |
| 1902 | 137 | 538 | 177 | 33 | 16 | 3 | 251 | 105 | 91 | 43 | .329 |
| 1903 | 129 | 512 | 182 | 30 | 19 | 5 | 265 | 97 | 101 | 44 | .355 |
| 1904 | 132 | 490 | 171 | 44 | 14 | 4 | 255 | 97 | 75 | 59 | .349 |
| 1905 | 147 | 548 | 199 | 32 | 14 | 6 | 277 | 114 | 101 | 54 | .363 |
| 1906 | 142 | 516 | 175 | 38 | 9 | 2 | 237 | 103 | 71 | 58 | .339 |
| 1907 | 142 | 515 | 180 | 38 | 14 | 6 | 264 | 98 | 82 | 46 | .350 |
| 1908 | 151 | 568 | 201 | 39 | 19 | 10 | 308 | 100 | 109 | 54 | .354 |
| 1909 | 137 | 495 | 168 | 39 | 10 | 5 | 242 | 92 | 100 | 66 | .339 |
| 1910 | 150 | 556 | 178 | 34 | 8 | 4 | 240 | 90 | 81 | 59 | .320 |
| 1911 | 130 | 473 | 158 | 23 | 16 | 9 | 240 | 87 | 89 | 67 | .334 |
| 1912 | 145 | 558 | 181 | 35 | 20 | 7 | 277 | 91 | 102 | 59 | .324 |
| 1913 | 114 | 413 | 124 | 18 | 4 | 3 | 159 | 51 | 56 | 26 | .300 |
| 1914 | 150 | 552 | 139 | 15 | 9 | 1 | 175 | 60 | 50 | 51 | .252 |
| 1915 | 151 | 566 | 155 | 32 | 17 | 6 | 239 | 68 | 78 | 39 | .274 |
| 1916 | 123 | 432 | 124 | 15 | 9 | 1 | 160 | 45 | 39 | 34 | .287 |
| 1917 | 74 | 230 | 61 | 7 | 1 | 0 | 70 | 15 | 24 | 24 | .265 |
| **TOTAL** | **2789** | **10449** | **3430** | **651** | **252** | **101** | **4888** | **1740** | **1732** | **963** | **.329** |

# TED WILLIAMS

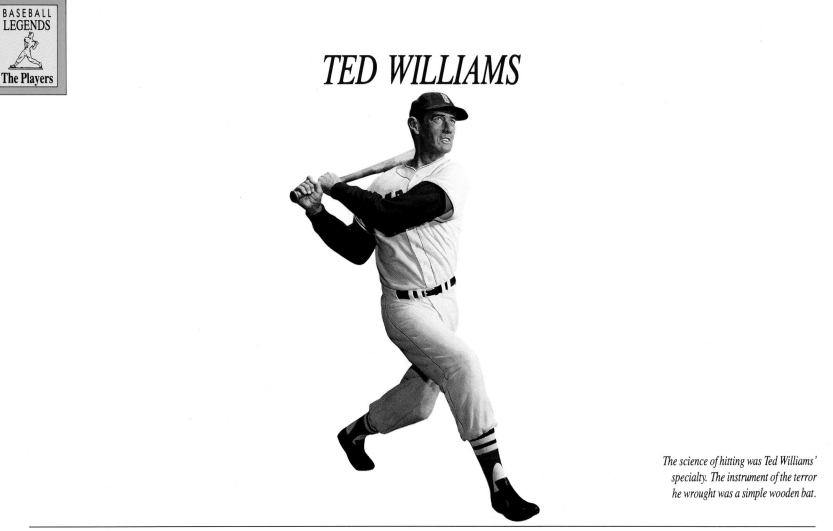

*The science of hitting was Ted Williams' specialty. The instrument of the terror he wrought was a simple wooden bat.*

*Williams led the American League in bases on balls for six straight seasons he appeared in, averaging 149 over that time.*

He was the consummate craftsman, a man who mastered the science and intimate subtleties of the strike zone, perhaps better than anyone before or since. So keen was the batting eye of Theodore Samuel Williams that if he took a pitch, umpires invariably called it a ball.

Williams, 6-foot-3 and only 160 pounds as a rookie out of San Diego, torched the major leagues in 1939 when he arrived in Boston. He led the American League in runs batted in with 145 (the best total ever for a rookie), hit .327, finished second in doubles (44), and third in home runs (31) with the second-highest rookie totals in history, and drew 107 walks, another first-year record. And then, against all odds, the left fielder raised the level of his overall game.

In 1941, Joe DiMaggio made the headlines with a 56-game hitting streak, but during the same period, "The Splendid Splinter" outhit DiMaggio .412 to .408. Williams produced 185 hits that season in 456 official at-bats, and that translated to a .406 average. No one has reached the .400 plateau since. Like DiMaggio's streak, it is a standard against which the best players are measured.

In the All-Star game that year, Williams hit a dramatic three-run home run with two out in the ninth off Claude Passeau of the National League. The American League won, 7-5, and Williams' greatness had been certified in a game that offered baseball's crème de la crème.

That .406 resulted in Williams' first batting title, but he would win five more. He won four home run titles and two triple crowns, in 1942 and 1947. Nine times, Williams led the league in slugging percentage. His place in baseball history is secure; Williams is among the career leaders in batting average, home runs, runs batted in, slugging percentage, and walks. This seems remarkable considering he missed nearly five full seasons due to military service and two major injuries.

Williams never seemed to lose the touch. In 1957, at 39, he batted .388 to lead the league and hit 38 home runs. The next year, his .328 average was again the best. In 1960, Williams appeared in 113 games for the Red Sox. He had never been a particular favorite of the fans there, who thought he was arrogant; Williams merely spoke the truth of his abilities. He hit 29 home runs in that farewell season, at the age of 42. The last came, appropriately, in his final game. And even Boston's stubborn fans had to rise to their feet in tribute. They knew they had seen a spectacular closing to a spectacular career.

| | S | | T | | A | | | T | | S | |
|---|---|---|---|---|---|---|---|---|---|---|---|
| **YEAR** | **G** | **AB** | **H** | **2B** | **3B** | **HR** | **TB** | **R** | **RBI** | **BB** | **AVG** |
| 1939 | 149 | 565 | 185 | 44 | 11 | 31 | 344 | 131 | 145 | 107 | .327 |
| 1940 | 144 | 561 | 193 | 43 | 14 | 23 | 333 | 134 | 113 | 96 | .344 |
| 1941 | 143 | 456 | 185 | 33 | 3 | 37 | 335 | 135 | 120 | 145 | .406 |
| 1942 | 150 | 522 | 186 | 34 | 5 | 36 | 338 | 141 | 137 | 145 | .356 |
| 1946 | 150 | 514 | 176 | 37 | 8 | 38 | 343 | 142 | 123 | 156 | .342 |
| 1947 | 156 | 528 | 181 | 40 | 9 | 32 | 335 | 125 | 114 | 162 | .343 |
| 1948 | 137 | 509 | 188 | 44 | 3 | 25 | 313 | 124 | 127 | 126 | .369 |
| 1949 | 155 | 566 | 194 | 39 | 3 | 43 | 368 | 150 | 159 | 162 | .343 |
| 1950 | 89 | 334 | 106 | 24 | 1 | 26 | 216 | 82 | 97 | 82 | .317 |
| 1951 | 148 | 531 | 169 | 28 | 4 | 30 | 295 | 109 | 126 | 144 | .318 |
| 1952 | 6 | 10 | 4 | 0 | 1 | 1 | 9 | 2 | 3 | 2 | .400 |
| 1953 | 37 | 91 | 37 | 6 | 0 | 13 | 82 | 17 | 34 | 19 | .407 |
| 1954 | 117 | 386 | 133 | 23 | 1 | 29 | 245 | 93 | 89 | 136 | .345 |
| 1955 | 98 | 320 | 114 | 21 | 3 | 28 | 225 | 77 | 83 | 91 | .356 |
| 1956 | 136 | 400 | 138 | 28 | 2 | 24 | 242 | 71 | 82 | 102 | .345 |
| 1957 | 132 | 420 | 163 | 28 | 1 | 38 | 307 | 96 | 87 | 119 | .388 |
| 1958 | 129 | 411 | 135 | 23 | 2 | 26 | 240 | 81 | 85 | 98 | .328 |
| 1959 | 103 | 272 | 69 | 15 | 0 | 10 | 114 | 32 | 43 | 52 | .254 |
| 1960 | 113 | 310 | 98 | 15 | 0 | 29 | 200 | 56 | 72 | 75 | .316 |
| **TOTAL** | **2292** | **7706** | **2654** | **525** | **71** | **521** | **4884** | **1798** | **1839** | **2019** | **.344** |

*He didn't look for accolades—and the Fenway Park crowds rarely offered them—but Ted Williams was one of the game's most consistently brilliant performers.*

*Quite simply, Cy Young is the standard against which all pitchers are measured. His 511 career victories may never be equaled.*

# CY YOUNG

*Young won more than 30 games five times in his 22-year career.*

Commissioner of Baseball Ford Frick had a problem in 1956. He was concerned that voters for the Most Valuable Player awards tended to choose only every-day players, overlooking pitchers who took the mound every four or five days. Frick eventually concluded that a separate award should be created. Now, what to name it?

One name loomed above all others. Cy Young's 511 career victories were easily the highest total in baseball history, and made Frick's choice an easy one. Now, the Cy Young Award is voted to the best pitcher in each league. And with good reason.

Denton True "Cy" Young was born in Gilmore, Ohio in 1867. Twenty-three years later, the strapping 6-foot-2, 210 pound right-hander went 9-7 for Cleveland of the National League. In 1891, he won 27 games and won more than 20 games each season for fourteen consecutive years. During that span he won 395 games, more than anyone managed in a career, with the exception of Walter Johnson. That works out to an average per-season record of 28-15.

Of course, today's critics say that Young's achievements must be viewed with cynicism, suggesting that the conditions of play back in 1890 were too different to permit meaningful comparison. In 1903, when major league baseball stabilized into its present form, Young was already 36 years old. Still, he put together seasons of 28-9 and 26-16. A few years later, Young won 22 games in 1907 and 21 in 1908—at the age of 41.

He proved himself again and again. Young remains baseball's only 200–game winner in both the National and American leagues. He won 20 games or more sixteen times and Young's 36 victories in 1892 came from 49 starting opportunities. His 35-win season in 1895 represented more than half of Cleveland's victories. Young lost only 10 games that year.

Overall, there were two no-hitters and on one improbable day, a perfect game against the Athletics in 1904 when he pitched 24 consecutive hitless innings. Imagine that. Young appeared in the very first World Series in 1903 and won two of three games.

Yet, the arguments endure. Young was clearly ahead of his time. Is there evidence that he wouldn't have dominated today's game? No. And as each new hurling phenom blazes across our consciousness of the national pastime, remember the standard against which he is historically judged. If he is acclaimed as the best for an entire season, he wins the Cy Young Award.

## S T A T S

| YEAR | G | W | L | IP | SO | TBB | GS | CG | ShO | ERA |
|---|---|---|---|---|---|---|---|---|---|---|
| 1890 | 17 | 9 | 7 | 148 | 39 | 30 | 16 | 16 | 0 | 3.47 |
| 1891 | 55 | 27 | 20 | 424 | 147 | 140 | 46 | 43 | 0 | 2.85 |
| 1892 | 53 | 36 | 11 | 453 | 168 | 118 | 49 | 48 | 9 | 1.93 |
| 1893 | 53 | 32 | 16 | 423 | 102 | 103 | 46 | 42 | 1 | 3.36 |
| 1894 | 52 | 25 | 22 | 409 | 108 | 106 | 47 | 44 | 2 | 3.94 |
| 1895 | 47 | 35 | 10 | 370 | 121 | 75 | 40 | 36 | 4 | 3.24 |
| 1896 | 51 | 29 | 16 | 414 | 140 | 62 | 46 | 42 | 5 | 3.24 |
| 1897 | 46 | 21 | 18 | 335 | 88 | 49 | 38 | 35 | 2 | 3.79 |
| 1898 | 46 | 25 | 14 | 378 | 101 | 41 | 41 | 40 | 1 | 2.53 |
| 1899 | 44 | 26 | 15 | 369 | 111 | 44 | 42 | 40 | 4 | 2.58 |
| 1900 | 41 | 20 | 18 | 321 | 115 | 36 | 35 | 32 | 4 | 3.00 |
| 1901 | 43 | 33 | 10 | 371 | 158 | 37 | 41 | 38 | 5 | 1.62 |
| 1902 | 45 | 32 | 10 | 385 | 160 | 53 | 43 | 41 | 3 | 2.15 |
| 1903 | 40 | 28 | 10 | 342 | 176 | 37 | 35 | 34 | 7 | 2.08 |
| 1904 | 43 | 26 | 16 | 380 | 200 | 29 | 41 | 40 | 10 | 1.97 |
| 1905 | 38 | 18 | 19 | 321 | 210 | 30 | 34 | 32 | 5 | 1.82 |
| 1906 | 39 | 13 | 21 | 288 | 140 | 25 | 34 | 28 | 0 | 3.19 |
| 1907 | 43 | 22 | 15 | 343 | 147 | 51 | 37 | 33 | 6 | 1.99 |
| 1908 | 36 | 21 | 11 | 299 | 150 | 37 | 33 | 30 | 3 | 1.26 |
| 1909 | 35 | 19 | 15 | 295 | 109 | 59 | 34 | 30 | 3 | 2.26 |
| 1910 | 21 | 7 | 10 | 163 | 58 | 27 | 20 | 14 | 1 | 2.53 |
| 1911 | 18 | 7 | 9 | 126 | 55 | 28 | 18 | 12 | 2 | 3.78 |
| **TOTAL** | **906** | **511** | **313** | **7357** | **2803** | **1217** | **816** | **750** | **77** | **2.63** |

TONY LAZZERI

BIG LEAGUE CHEWING GUM

# Alexander Strikes Out Lazzeri

It was a classic confrontation, heightened by the stark contrast of the players involved. In the batter's box at Yankee Stadium stood Tony Lazzeri, a rookie of 23. Thirty-nine-year-old St. Louis Cardinals pitcher Grover Cleveland Alexander, in his 15th major league campaign, scowled at him from the mound. The date was October 9, 1926, and it was the seventh game of the World Series with the Cardinals ahead 3-2 in the seventh inning and the bases loaded.

To that point, the Yankees' young second baseman had distinguished himself by leading the American League with 96 strikeouts. Still, he had knocked in 114 runs for his trouble and was installed as the Yankees' sixth hitter, behind Babe Ruth and Lou Gehrig. Alexander had seen considerably more of the baseball world, with tours of duty in Philadelphia and Chicago. The Cubs procured him from the Athletics in 1917 for two players and $55,000. Alexander, who had averaged 27 wins for seven years in Philadelphia, cooled off in Chicago. On June 22, 1926, the Cardinals picked him up for the modest waiver price and Alexander responded with 9 victories in 16 decisions.

Each player had experienced success in the Series before they squared off in the ultimate game. Alexander struck out 10 batters in the second game and won a 6-2 decision. Lazzeri's sacrifice fly in the tenth inning of the fifth game gave the Yankees a 3-2 Series edge, and Alexander responded with a 10-2 victory in the imperative sixth game.

The Cardinals' one-run lead in the seventh game was in jeopardy when Alexander was called into the game. With the bases loaded, the crowd of 38,093 was screaming. Rogers Hornsby, the St. Louis manager and great Hall of Fame hitter, who had envisioned such a scenario and asked Alexander to limit his celebrating the night before, wanted his ace to pitch to Lazzeri. Alexander needed only three warm-up pitches. A day earlier, Alexander had stopped Lazzeri four times with curve balls, so he threw another one—strike one. Lazzeri drilled an ill-advised fastball down the left field line, foul by only a foot—strike two. Another hard-breaking curve slammed into the glove of catcher Bob O'Farrell, leaving Lazzeri flat-footed, facing Alexander on the mound—strike three.

The rest was anti-climactic. Alexander pitched the last two innings and not many remember that the game ended when Ruth tried to steal second base. Instead, baseball fans remember the day the Cardinals beat the Yankees, and experience conquered youth.

*Fred Snodgrass had a serviceable bat, as his lifetime batting average of .275 indicates. It was his glove, however, which lives in infamy.*

# Snodgrass' Big Mistake

**M**ost of baseball's greatest games revolve around heroic feats: Bobby Thomson's monumental home run, Don Larsen's perfect game, Hank Aaron's 755th home run. And there are the unfortunates like New York Giants outfielder Fred Snodgrass, whose name lives in infamy, unless of course you are a Boston Red Sox fan.

Before October 16, 1912, Snodgrass had done little to dishonor himself. In fact, the 5-foot-11, 175-pound center fielder had batted .321 two years earlier and maintained respectable production numbers. Over the regular season in 1912, for instance, Snodgrass scored a career-high 91 runs and knocked in 69 more. He was an adequate outfielder.

The Red Sox and Giants found themselves in the World Series, having obliterated their respective leagues; Boston's 105-47 record was 14 games better than second-place Washington and New York's 103-48 mark bested Pittsburgh by 10. "Smokey" Joe Wood of the Red Sox and the Giants' Rube Marquard had each won two games of the entertaining matchup that stood at three games each. The Series' final game was actually the eighth game between the two teams as the second game had been called on account of darkness with the score tied 6-6 in eleven innings.

After nine exhausting innings in the deciding game, the score was tied at 1-1. The Giants pushed ahead 2-1 in the top of the tenth when Red Murray doubled off Wood and Tris Speaker momentarily juggled Fred Merkle's single to center field. With the great, untiring Christy Mathewson on the mound for New York, the game appeared over. It was at this time that Snodgrass blundered his way into baseball history.

Batting for Wood, Clyde Engle stroked a towering fly toward center. Both Murray and Snodgrass moved for the ball, but Snodgrass called for it. Perhaps he was still thinking about his leadoff out back in the top of the ninth, or maybe Murray's close presence interrupted his concentration. Whatever, the ball hit Snodgrass' glove and then dropped out. Engle arrived safely at second, amazed at his good fortune. Snodgrass atoned partially for the error by robbing the next hitter—Harry Hooper—of an extra-base hit in deep center field. Then Mathewson, still clearly agitated over Snodgrass' blunder, walked Steve Yerkes on four pitches. Like Engle, Speaker was granted a huge favor when the Giants allowed his pop foul to fall harmlessly among three players. He singled on Mathewson's next pitch and delivered Engle home. After Duffy Lewis was walked intentionally, Larry Gardner lofted a long fly to right field and the Red Sox had won the Series. Or, as historians have noted, Snodgrass had lost it.

*In 1920, the league-leading Brooklyn Robins (above) battled the relentless Boston Braves in a record-setting 26-inning marathon. The game ended in a 1-1 tie, when it was finally called on account of darkness.*

# The Longest Game

It was the baseball game that wouldn't end, a 26-inning odyssey that stands today as the longest ever played.

On paper, at least, the May 1, 1920 contest didn't figure. The Brooklyn Robins were on their way to a spectacular 93-61 season and a berth in the World Series. The Boston Braves were destined to finish 30 games back, at 62-90. But for that one day, all things were equal and the two teams finished in a 1-1 tie. No runs were scored in the last twenty innings and, incredibly, both pitchers went the distance. That was their sole gift to history because Joe Oeschger and Leon Cadore each finished modest careers with losing records.

Oeschger, a fastballer, had already distinguished himself the year before by playing for three teams, finishing the season with Boston. Cadore, who threw a curveball, was in his sixth season with the Robins. Oeschger gave in first: catcher Ernie Krueger received one of the pitcher's rare (three) free passes to lead off the fifth, Cadore advanced Krueger to second with a fielder's choice back to Oeschger, and leadoff hitter Ivy Olson knocked in the game's first run with a single to left.

The Braves stormed back in the sixth to tie it when right fielder Walt Cruise reached

Cadore for a triple and Tony Boeckel subsequently singled to center. In retrospect, it seems convenient to blame the arm of center fielder Wally Hood for the length of the evening. His throw cut down Boeckel at the plate moments later when he tried to score on a double by shortstop Rabbitt Maranville. And that, quite simply, was that.

It was not without a few scares, though. Brooklyn left fielder Zack Wheat saved a certain extra-base hit with a terrific running catch at the wall. Later, in the 17th inning, the Robins loaded the bases with one out, but Oeschger induced catcher Rowdy Elliot to ground back to the mound and Wheat was forced at the plate. Walter Holke, who tried to score when catcher Hank Gowdy attempted to throw Elliott out at first, was thrown out at home by Brooklyn first baseman Ed Konetchy.

After nearly four hours, umpire Barry McCormick had seen enough—or couldn't see enough, with darkness rapidly moving in. He declared an end to the proceedings one inning short of a total effort equivalent to three regular games. In 1984, the Milwaukee Brewers and Chicago White Sox would play a 25-inning game, but it would only serve to underline the epic nature of that struggle 64 years before.

# Harvey Haddix'
# *Perfect Loss*

N o, the world isn't a fair place. Just ask Harvey Haddix, baseball's best example of a man unfairly wronged.

On May 26, 1959, there was no justice for the Pittsburgh Pirates' left-hander. Haddix pitched 12 perfect innings, retired 36 straight batters—and lost to the Milwaukee Braves 1-0 in a thirteen inning game in which the Pirates outhit the Braves 12-1.

The 19,194 fans at Milwaukee's County Stadium could not have been expecting it. At 33, Haddix' best seasons were already behind him. He had won 20 games for St. Louis in 1953, but the Pirates were his fourth team in four years and he was destined to finish the season at a middling 12-12. Lew Burdette was on the mound for Milwaukee, a right-hander. He would be less effective than Haddix, if only from an artistic standpoint.

As Haddix ripped through the Braves' predominantly right-handed lineup with fastballs and sliders, Burdette worked in and out of jams of his own doing. Haddix only flirted with danger twice, and each time shortstop Dick Schofield was fast enough to get Milwaukee shortstop Johnny Logan out. Schofield left his feet to snare Logan's third-inning line drive and in the sixth went deep into the hole between shortstop and third base, came up with the ball, and threw Logan out at first.

The two-out hitter in the ninth, Burdette didn't mind telling Haddix that he was going to break up the no-hit bid. It didn't happen; Burdette missed a two-and-two slider and traditional baseball history-making had been set on its head. Never before had a perfect nine-inning game been thrown without a victory going to the successful pitcher. And as the game progressed the fans backed Haddix more and more with every perfect inning. When he escaped the eleventh, Haddix became the first pitcher to throw a no-hitter of that duration.

Haddix, who stood only 5-foot-9 and weighed 170 pounds, seemed to tire in the twelfth inning. In the unlucky thirteenth, Felix Mantilla became the first Milwaukee baserunner when third baseman Don Hoak took his grounder and threw wildly past first. Eddie Mathews bunted Mantilla to second and slugger Hank Aaron was intentionally passed. The next hitter, first baseman Joe Adcock, had failed to hit the ball out of the infield in four previous at-bats, but he caught a weak slider up in the strike zone and drove it over the fence in right-center for a home run and a 3-0 victory for Milwaukee—or so it seemed. Aaron, however, thought the ball hit at the base of the fence and therefore figured Mantilla had already scored the winning run. He headed toward the Braves' dugout and Adcock ran right past him. Aaron tried to retrace his steps but the next day National League president Warren Giles ruled the official score was 1-0. This was small consolation for Haddix, who, understandably, felt perfectly awful.

*Harvey Haddix pitched for St. Louis five seasons, then spent a year each in Philadelphia and Cincinnati before going to the Bucs.*

*When baseball fans call up memories,*
*Game Six of the 1975 World Series is*
*invariably near the top of the list.*

# *1975 World Series, Game Six*

There are sometimes games in baseball that transcend the sport itself. On October 21, 1975, the Boston Red Sox and Cincinnati Reds played such a game. Some experts feel it was the greatest game in the greatest World Series in history. Certainly, the 35,205 fans jammed into Fenway Park and the 70 million at home watching on television will never forget it.

It was Cincinnati's Big Red Machine, featuring Pete Rose, Johnny Bench, Joe Morgan, George Foster, and Tony Perez, against the Red Sox, who were trying to recapture the Impossible Dream of 1967 with a cast of characters that included Luis Tiant, Carl Yastrzemski, and Rico Petrocelli. Boston trailed 3-2 in the Series and faced extinction because Perez had ended an 0-15 streak in dramatic fashion by hitting two home runs in the previous game.

After a five-day rain delay, the Red Sox, playing as though their lives depended on it, jumped out to a 3-0 lead in the first inning. Center fielder Fred Lynn hoisted a Gary Nolan pitch into the darkness and the fans in Boston dared to believe in miracles. Tiant, the only Red Sox pitcher to beat the Reds so far, had drawn this critical mound assignment. In the Cincinnati fifth, Tiant looked vulnerable when right fielder Ken Griffey tripled off the wall in center, just over the head of a diving Lynn who also bounced off the wall. That scored Ed Armbrister and Rose, who had reached previously on a walk and a single. Bench's single delivered Griffey with the tying run.

Cincinnati took a 5-3 lead in the seventh inning when Foster doubled and added another run in the eighth on a solo home run by Cesar Geronimo. At that point, El Tiante was asked to leave and it looked like the Boston fans would be disappointed yet again. Yet in the bottom half of the inning pinch-hitter Bernie Carbo stepped to the plate with Lynn and Petrocelli on base. Rawly Eastwick seemed to have Carbo jammed on a three-two fastball, but Carbo got enough to foul the ball off. The next pitch, a pretty fair fastball, landed 400 feet away over the center field fence. Now knotted at 6-6, a great game became greater. And greater with each inning.

Foster nailed Boston second baseman Denny Doyle at the plate in the ninth inning, and in the eleventh Red Sox right fielder Dwight Evans took a home run away from Morgan with a splendid leaping catch and completed a double play by throwing to first. Then, at 12:35 a.m., Boston catcher Carlton Fisk provided the only possible climax to a game of such magnitude. He faced Cincinnati's eighth pitcher, Pat Darcy, and hit his one-ball offering down the left field line. And there was Fisk, all boyish innocence, waving the ball fair with both arms. Mouth open, he watched the wind push the ball back into play, barely, and into the great screen over left field. He jumped for joy and circled the bases with glee.

The Red Sox would lose the seventh game a night later, 4-3, on Morgan's two-out single in the ninth, but something—everything—that had touched Game Six was missing in that contest.

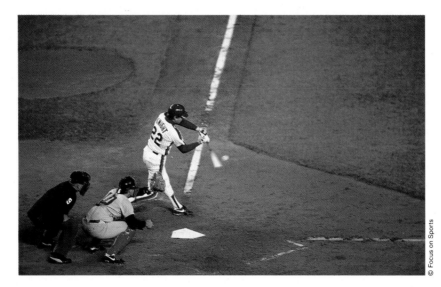

# 1986 World Series, Game Six

Even the most fatalistic Red Sox fan could allow himself a little room to breathe, a moment at last to ponder the wonder of a World Series championship. Victory would be Boston's this year. In 1967, undermanned Boston had played St. Louis courageously only to lose in the seventh game; in 1975, the Red Sox staged a heroic victory in Game Six before Cincinnati asserted itself and won the Series in the seventh. Now, on October 25th, in the sixth game of the 1986 World Series, Boston pitcher Calvin Schiraldi was a single tenth-inning strike away from ending the New York Mets' season.

Yet, somehow it got away. Again. The Mets, going to a two strike count with three different hitters, put together three singles, then took advantage of a wild pitch by pitcher Bob Stanley and an error by first baseman Bill Buckner to score three runs and win a pulsating 6-5 game at Shea Stadium.

So the Red Sox fulfilled conclusively, it seemed, their role as a team of tragic fate. New York scored all eight of its runs in the last three innings of the seventh game to wrap up the title, 8-5. And the Red Sox were left to wonder how it happened.

Only two weeks earlier, they had been on the other side of agony. The California Angels were themselves a strike away from the World Series when center fielder Dave Henderson hit a home run that eventually carried Boston into extra innings. He drove home the winning run, 7-6, in the eleventh with a sacrifice fly. And so the curse of Angel manager Gene Mauch—that he would never manage in the World Series—was also confirmed.

Henderson had eight hits in the first five games against the Mets, including a triple in the Red Sox 4-2 victory that preceded their ignominious fate in Game Six. He dealt the Mets another blow leading off the tenth inning of that contest with a solo home run. Second baseman Marty Barrett singled home third baseman Wade Boggs to make it 5-3. Schiraldi set down second baseman Wally Backman and first baseman Keith Hernandez on outfield flies. In Hernandez' mind the contest was over, so dejectedly he retired to manager Davey Johnson's office, opened a beer, and watched the game on television. Here is what he saw:

Catcher Gary Carter singled and pinch-hitter Kevin Mitchell hit a two-and-two pitch to follow suit. Ray Knight (who would later be named the Series' Most Valuable Player), faced a two-strike count and also singled. That scored Carter and moved Mitchell to third. Center fielder Mookie Wilson worked the count to two and two, then fouled off two pitches. Mitchell scored when Boston catcher Rich Gedman couldn't stop Stanley's wild pitch to tie the game at 5-5. Then Wilson sent a little bouncer in the direction of Buckner, who lifted his glove prematurely. The ball got behind him and Knight scored the winning run as 55,078 partisans bellowed.

"The ball went skip, skip and it didn't come up," Buckner said later. "The ball missed my glove. I've got to live with it." The same goes for Red Sox fans.

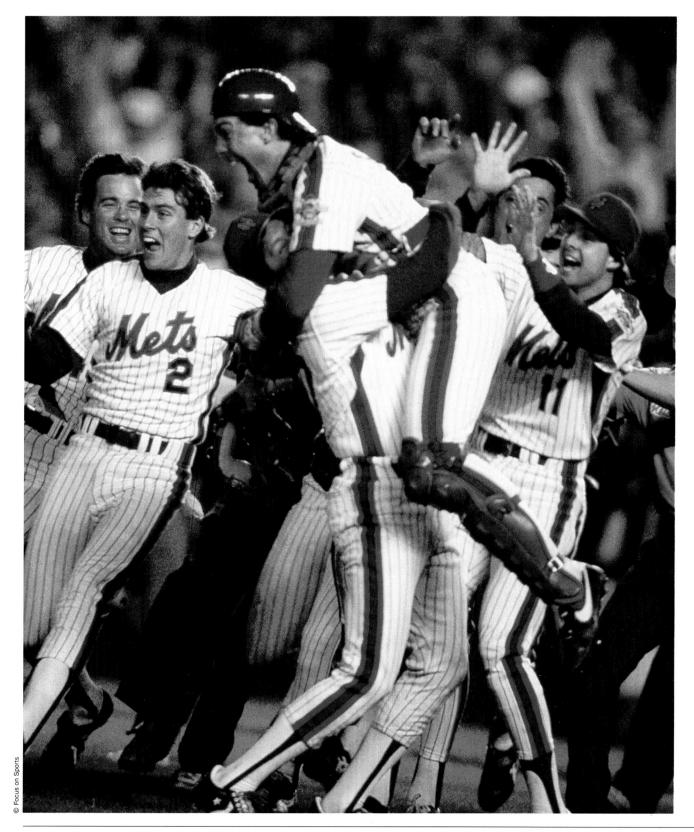

A strike away from elimination,
the Mets came back to defeat
the Red Sox in heroic fashion.
Ray Knight, far left, singled to keep
the threat alive in the tenth
inning. He later scored the
improbable winning run and
catcher Gary Carter celebrated
with winning pitcher Jesse
Orosco.

*Vic Wertz will never know how Willie*
*Mays caught up to this ball.*

# Willie Mays' Great Catch

I t might have been baseball's greatest catch of all time. That it came at an important time (the eighth inning of a 2-2 contest), in an important game (the first of the 1954 World Series), by an important player (Willie Mays) only made it greater still.

The New York Giants, having held off the Brooklyn Dodgers down the stretch of the season, met the Cleveland Indians, whose record in the American League was 14 games better and itself a record, at 111-43. The Tribe was favored overwhelmingly to handle the Giants, but throughout the Series, Mays simply did not allow defeat. In the first inning of Game 1, Vic Wertz' triple off Sal Maglie gave the Indians a 2-0 lead at the Polo Grounds. Maglie eventually regained his celebrated control and found himself in a 2-2 game after third baseman Hank Thompson singled home two runs in the bottom of the third.

It was still tied when Cleveland centerfielder Larry Doby worked Maglie for a walk to open the eighth inning. Third baseman Al Rosen followed with an infield hit, bringing to the plate Wertz, who had singled twice in addition to his triple. With that in mind, Giants manager Leo Durocher brought in left-hander Don Liddle to pitch. The first pitch was crushed toward deep center field, a 460-foot smash. But Mays, who had been playing

customarily shallow, turned and bolted straight for the wall. A few feet away, Mays reached out at full speed, both hands extended, and caught the ball. He turned and threw in one motion, holding Doby at second. Liddle got the next two batters and instead of trailing 4-2, the Giants were still alive.

"Had it all the way," Mays said stepping into the dugout. The same was true of the play he made on Wertz in the tenth inning that was, in many ways, just as scintillating as the eighth-inning catch. Wertz hit a blast to left-center and Mays, running again at full tilt, just managed to stab the ball back-handed and so held Wertz to a double. "It was the toughest chance I had the entire Series," Mays said later, with no apologies to the historians.

With Mays on second base in the bottom of the tenth, by virtue of a walk and stolen base and Hank Thompson standing on first after an intentional walk, "Dusty" Rhodes hit Bob Lemon's hanging curve down the left field line, a scant 258 feet from the plate. That was enough to get it over the fence, however, and the Giants won the Series' first game, 5-2. And though Rhodes was to be the offensive hero in New York's four-game sweep, Mays' glove had allowed it to be.

*Note the look of awe on the catcher's face. Note the umpire's smile. Babe Ruth has just crossed the plate after his legendary shot and even teammate Lou Gehrig couldn't believe it.*

# *Babe Ruth's Called Home Run*

By Oct. 1, 1932, Babe Ruth's place in history was already secure. He had hit 648 of his astounding 714 home runs, made a lot of money, and produced enough baseball legend and lore to fill several archives. Why then, on this particular autumn day, was the pride of the New York Yankees circling the bases with a grin on his broad face? Why were the fans of the Chicago Cubs rising to their feet at Wrigley Field?

"I just laughed, laughed to myself going around the bases and was thinking what a lucky bum I was," Ruth would say later. For his fifth-inning World Series home run off the Cubs' Charlie Root, a smash to center field that proved to be the longest ball ever hit at Wrigley Field, provided his happiest moment in baseball. More than that, the story would amplify Ruth's greatness as a larger-than-life hero.

It had been a lively Series even before this third game. The invectives had been flowing freely from both dugouts since the Cubbies had voted former Yankee Mark Koenig only a half share of their playoff money after he was brought up from the minors—and since the Yankees took great pains to point out Chicago's penurious ways. Ruth, who never liked to miss any fun, was in the middle of it all.

As Ruth stepped up to the plate in the first inning, Cubs trainer Andy Lotshaw cracked,

"If I had you on my team, I'd hitch you to a wagon," referring to the Bambino's comfortable midsection. Shouts of "Big Belly" and "Balloon Head," followed Ruth to the plate. He promptly took Root to deep center field for a three-run home run.

It was a 4-4 game in the fifth when Ruth called his famous home run. Or didn't. What happened was this: Loosing another barrage of verbiage, the Chicago bench jockeys were rewarded with a disdaining choke sign from Ruth. Then Root quickly threw two called strikes and Ruth raised his index finger, saying, "I still have one left." And the Chicago bench roared. Now, the question of whether Ruth actually pointed to the center field fence or merely waved his finger back at Root, standing sullen on the mound, has never been satisfactorily answered. No matter, Ruth buried the next pitch in the center field seats with a powerful, sweeping swing. It landed roughly where his finger seemed to have pointed and rendered the Cubs silent as Ruth bowed deeply to their dugout as he rounded third. Chicago lost the Series in four straight and the nation gained a delicious piece of history.

"I could have struck out just as well as not because I was mad and I'd made up my mind to swing at the next pitch if I could reach it with a bat," Ruth said later. "When I think of the good breaks in my life—that was one of them."

*Never mind that Mets baserunner J.C. Martin is running in fair territory illegally. The throw hit him in the shoulder and the Mets went on to win the World Series against the Orioles.*

# The Amazin' Mets Of 1969

The 1962 New York Mets were a bad joke. They lost the first nine games in the franchise's history and ultimately finished with a dubious 40-120 record, some 60½ games behind San Francisco in the National League. There was a 17-game losing streak somewhere around Memorial Day and Sandy Koufax blew them away with a no-hitter a month later. Marv Throneberry, who came to New York from the Baltimore Orioles in May, hit .244, his second-best season in the majors, and committed a league-leading 17 errors at first base. Pitcher Roger Craig, bless him, lost 24 games.

Yet for some reason, New Yorkers took to Casey Stengel's bedraggled Mutts. Perhaps it was the radical chic of the times to invest emotionally in a lost cause, or maybe it was just the hot dogs, but 922,530 flocked to the Polo Grounds. The 51-111 Mets finished 48 games out in 1963 and more than a million passed through the doors in New York's last season at the Polo Grounds. The change of venue lifted the Mets to a lofty 53-109 a year later at Shea Stadium. Clearly, these Mets were going somewhere. Just where, no one was quite sure.

This backdrop of futility is necessary to appreciate the Mets' unlikely accomplishment in 1969. They had finished ninth the year before, with a record of 73-89. It would never happen again, because the new concept of divisional play wouldn't allow it. Now, the Mets were part of the National League's East Division—and when the regular season was over they were the best part of it.

Tom Seaver (25-7) captured his first Cy Young Award and nearly threw a perfect game against the Chicago Cubs; the Mets won 11 consecutive games through the straits of Memorial Day; and Cleon Jones carried the New York offense with a .340 batting average. It wasn't easy, however. This was, after all, the Mets. They trailed the Cubs by 9½ games on August 13, then won 38 of 49 to take the East title by eight games. The Atlanta Braves succumbed in three straight playoff games, but not many experts gave the Mets a chance against the Orioles in the World Series.

Baltimore, 109-53 in the American League, had a great pitching staff, featuring Jim Palmer, Dave McNally, and Mike Cuellar, as well as a pair of Hall of Fame Robinsons, Frank and Brooks. When Don Buford hit Seaver's second pitch of the opener for a home run, a lot of people nodded knowingly. The Orioles went on to win that first game, and the series seemed over before it was over. And then something truly amazing happened—the Mets.

They won four straight games. Ed Charles, Jerry Grote, and Al Weis all hit two-out singles in the ninth to win Game Two, 2-1; Tommy Agee and Ron Swoboda made spectacular catches as the Mets prevailed 5-0 and 2-1 in the third and fourth games. They trailed 3-0 in the final game but scored five runs in the last three innings and Shea Stadium erupted. Amazin'!

*The greeting at the plate was a fitting welcome for a hero of Bill Mazeroski's magnitude.*

# Bill Mazeroski's Home Run

That the Pittsburgh Pirates even lasted into the seventh game of the 1960 World Series was accomplishment enough, considering the weight of the evidence against them. Through six games, the New York Yankees had beaten the Bucs by the combined score of 46-17—including nasty victories of 16-3, 10-0, and 12-0—and outhit them 78 to 49. Yet somehow, Pittsburgh had survived to play on that October 13th.

So had Bill Mazeroski, the second baseman from Wheeling, West Virginia. He, like most of the spectators in the stands, knew the Pirates hadn't won a world championship in 35 years. In the sixth inning, it looked like Pittsburgh's chances of going 0-for-36 were quite good. An early 4-0 lead evaporated when the Yankees scored a run in the fifth and four more in the sixth. Catcher Yogi Berra's three-run homer was the big blow. New York made it 7-4 with two more runs in the top of the eighth.

The Pirates scratched their way back into the game, taking advantage of Gino Cimoli's single and Bill Virdon's sharp ground ball that hit shortstop Tony Kubek in the throat. Instead of two outs and no one on, Pittsburgh was in business with men at first and second.

Dick Groat's single scored Cimoli and Bob Skinner moved the runners up. Then, after Rocky Nelson flied to Roger Maris in right, Roberto Clemente reached base on an infield hit that scored Virdon. It was now 7-6. Backup catcher Hal Smith gave Pittsburgh a 9-7 lead when he zeroed in on a Jim Coates offering and drove it out for a three-run homer. The Yankees then tied it in the ninth when Bobby Richardson and pinch-hitter Dale Long led off with singles. Richardson scored on a single by Mickey Mantle and pinch-runner Gil Mc-Dougald ran home on Berra's smash down the first base line.

Ralph Terry, New York's big right-hander, would try to force the game into extra innings. For some reason, he threw a high fastball to the leadoff hitter, Mazeroski, a noted crusher of fastballs. The second baseman noted its location and turned on the next pitch, a similar effort pitched slightly lower. Mazeroski was still pumping his arms wildly and bearing down on second base when the roar of the crowd told him the ball had cleared the wall in left-center. He fairly skipped home through the frenzied fans and the Pirates were 10-9 winners. And Mazeroski was the man of a moment that still endures.

*You are pitcher Bob Cain and this is your assignment: Throw three pitches to this strike zone that may be a cubic foot in size.*

# Bill Veeck's Small Experiment

This is the story of Eddie Gaedel and how Bill Veeck, who always had a flair for the bizarre, made him the smallest big-leaguer ever.

Veeck had bought the St. Louis Browns in July, 1951 and immediately set about turning the woeful franchise around. The Browns had finished last or close to it almost every season. The fans disappeared, and Sportsman's Park became a ghost town. So Veeck brought creaking Satchel Paige over from the Cleveland Indians and, because the pitcher was forty-five years old, gave him the best seat in the house—a rocking chair in the bullpen. There were other flourishes: Marty Marion and Harry Breecheen, who as former Cardinals had marquee value, were added as coaches and the fabulous Dizzy Dean was placed behind the microphone.

Under the guise of a double birthday extravaganza—the American League and the Browns' beer sponsor, Falstaff, were celebrating—Veeck sprung his most (in)famous promotional trap. More than 18,000 fans were lured into Sportsman's Park on that August 18th and the Browns, true to form, lost the first game of a doubleheader to the Detroit Tigers. Between games there was a parade of sorts and a cake-cutting ceremony. And out of a seven-foot cake popped Eddie Gaedel, a forty-three-inch, 65-pound midget.

Veeck had booked him through a theatrical agent in Chicago and brought him very quietly to St. Louis where he was dressed in a child's baseball uniform emblazoned with the number $1/8$. When Gaedel stepped into the batter's box to lead off for St. Louis in the bottom of the first, umpire Ed Hurley, figuring the halftime show should have been long over, tried to throw him out. But a valid major-league contract was displayed and Gaedel settled in to await Bob Cain's first pitch, waving his toy bat menacingly.

Down in a crouch, Gaedel offered a strike zone of about a square foot, which wasn't nearly big enough for the flustered Cain. Four straight balls sailed in to catcher Bob Swift and Gaedel, who had been instructed by Veeck to resist swinging at anything, pranced to first base. When a pinch-runner was sent in, Gaedel waved his tiny cap to the now delirious crowd. One day later, the baseball purists predictably moved to ban midgets from further play. But the memory of Eddie Gaedel lingers. You can still find him today in the *Baseball Encyclopedia*, tucked in between Len Gabrielson and Gary Gaetti.

*There it goes…kiss that baby goodbye.*
*Roger Maris' 61st homer in the 1961*
*season produced dramatically*
*controversial results.*

# Roger Maris' 61st*
# Home Run

The asterisk is gone now, but the scars Roger Maris suffered remain in the memory of all who love baseball. In 1961 he challenged—and conquered—the most hallowed of baseball's single-season records: Babe Ruth's 60-home run mark. And he suffered a lot of grief for his considerable effort.

Maris was a 27-year-old right fielder who had shown a flair for hitting home runs in his first season with the Yankees. He was the American League's Most Valuable Player in 1960, with 39 homers and 112 runs batted in. Maris didn't lead the league that year—Mickey Mantle, in a stout display of one-upmanship, finished the year with 40—but he would in 1961, the first year of the expanded schedule. When Ruth had worn pinstripes in 1927, he set the record in 154 games. Now, the American League would play 162 games.

Maris, a 6-foot, 197-pounder, started slowly. His first home run from the left side of the plate came in the season's eleventh game off Paul Foytack of Detroit. And then Maris got hot; he hit 11 homers in May and added 15 more in June. By July 1st, Maris had hit 28 home runs, compared to Mantle's 27. He was also five games ahead of Ruth's pace. As the season lengthened so did the lines at Maris' locker. Sportswriters wanted to know his feelings as he hunted down "The Bambino." Maris, who had always guarded his privacy zealously, didn't handle it well. In truth, he had never had good press and the record chase merely exacerbated the situation.

As Maris stroked his way through July, adding 13 more home runs, the baseball establishment grew nervous. Commissioner Ford Frick decreed that Maris would not officially break Ruth's record unless he did it in the same 154 games Ruth had. Thus the potential asterisk was introduced. It haunted Maris to the very end of the season.

He had already tied Ruth on September 26, homering against Baltimore's Jack Fisher and now his last chance would come at Yankee Stadium against Boston on October 1. A crowd of 23,154 watched Maris fly weakly to left off rookie Tracy Stallard in the first inning. In the fourth, Maris stepped in again and drilled Stallard's two-ball pitch 10 rows into the right field stands. The fans understandably went wild. Maris trotted around the bases and, approaching the dugout, found his way blocked. His teammates forced him into four hat-waving encores before they relented.

The debate persists, unfairly, to this day. Should Maris get credit for the record? Certainly he played in 10 more games than Ruth did in his historic season and had 50 more at-bats. Yet, no one has hit 61 home runs before or since Maris—and that speaks for itself.

*After the big blast, Aaron had everything—the record, the ball, and a hug from his wife.*

# Hank Aaron's 715th Home Run

The politicians had already had their say: Hank Aaron was baseball's community property and therefore the Atlanta Braves' left fielder would play the opening series of the 1974 season at Cincinnati. Ordinarily there wouldn't have been such a fuss, but this was history and baseball commissioner Bowie Kuhn insisted it be shared with the rest of the National League.

Aaron had been intently cracking home runs through the years—713 through twenty seasons—leading up to this spring of incredible attention. That, of course, left him one shy of Babe Ruth's career record and when the Braves made noises about saving him for Atlanta Stadium, Kuhn stepped in. Sure enough, Aaron, a graceful 6-foot, 180-pound package from Mobile, Alabama, took his first swing at a Jack Billingham pitch and lost it 400 feet away, far over the left-center field wall at Riverfront Stadium. The nation discussed Aaron's home run number 714 with vigor for four days.

On April 8th, a crowd of 53,775 crammed into Atlanta Stadium hoping this would be the

night that Aaron would make them witness to another dramatic milestone in baseball's grand tradition. The bright lights of national television followed his every move, but Aaron refused to blink. He led off the second inning against the Los Angeles Dodgers with a walk. Pitcher Al Downing, whose unhappy lot it was to pitch the game and potentially become the wrong half of a trivia answer, followed a one-and-one count with three straight balls. The crowd was not amused.

Aaron, looking older than his forty years, returned to the plate in the fourth inning with Darrell Evans standing on first. Downing threw another ball, his fourth straight. Then, at 9:07 p.m., Aaron took his first swing of the night. It was the only one he needed. He delivered Downing's fastball over the wall in left field and into the glove of reliever Tom House, who was standing in the Braves' bullpen.

There it was: 715. Yet it fails to convey the enormity of the task achieved. Aaron, who finished his career with 755 home runs, nearly 33 a season for 23 years. How about that?

# The End Of Joe DiMaggio's 56-Game Streak

I f taking a round bat and a round ball and trying to hit it square is the most difficult singular feat in sport, then what to make of Joe DiMaggio's 56-game hitting streak from May 15 to July 16, 1941? Call it the greatest sports accomplishment through the ages and you won't be far from wrong.

It began harmlessly enough when the New York Yankees' center fielder singled in four plate appearances against Edgar Smith, a left-hander for the Chicago White Sox. On May 14, DiMaggio had taken the collar, going 0-for-3 against the Cleveland Indians' Mel Harder, who would only pitch 69 innings that year. At the time, New York was idling along at .500 after a disappointing third-place finish in 1940. DiMaggio had led the American League in hitting that year with a .352 average and he would surpass that figure in this magnificent season.

The first milestone DiMaggio passed was Rogers Hornsby's National League record of hitting in 33 consecutive games. In Washington, DiMaggio caught and passed George Sisler, who had held the American League record of 41. The last hurdle was Wee Willie Keeler's nineteenth-century mark of 44 and Boston's Heber Newsome obliged DiMaggio, yielding a homer that ran his streak to 45. The string stood at 56 games when a crowd of 67,468 turned out at Cleveland's Municipal Stadium on July 17th.

The Indians had been the last team to shut DiMaggio down and left-handed starter Al Smith seemed to be continuing the trend with some help from Ken Keltner at the hot corner. Keltner turned two DiMaggio smashes down the third-base line into outs with terrific back-handed stops. Smith had walked DiMaggio the second time he batted. DiMaggio's fourth and last chance came against Jim Bagby, a right-hander who would finish his career with a 97-96 record. The bases were loaded and there was one out in the eighth when DiMaggio lashed a shot to shortstop. Lou Boudreau, seeing the ball take a bad bounce, grabbed it with his bare hand and shoveled it to second baseman Ray Mack, who relayed it to first for a double-play.

*A fiercely determined Joe DiMaggio set baseball's most unassailable record.*

DiMaggio would go on to hit the next 16 straight games and finish the season with a batting average of .357. And the Yankees would ride into first place along with him. During DiMaggio's 56-game streak, New York won 41 games and went on to clinch an early pennant and take a five game World Series from the Brooklyn Dodgers. The record still stands today and may last as long as baseball itself.

# Bill Wambsganss' Unassisted Triple Play

Timing, they say, is everything. Consider the very special case of William Adolph Wambsganss, who placed himself as the right man in the right place at the right time to make some overwhelming World Series history on October 10, 1920.

Wambsganss was never known as an extaordinary player during his 13 years in the American League. The second baseman's career batting average was .259 and his fielding usually proved adequate. This was to be his one and only Series and Wambsganss would make it count. The stage was set as the Brooklyn Robins and Wambsganss' Cleveland Indians, tied at two games each, headed into Game Five at League Park.

In the first inning Indians' outfielder Elmer Smith hit the first grand slam in World Series history. It was still 4-0 in the fourth when Jim Bagby made his bid for the record books and took a Burleigh Grimes spitball into the center field bleachers. It was the first Series home run by a pitcher and gave Bagby a comfortable working margin of 7-0. And no one would

ever remember this game if Wambsganss hadn't forced himself into the scenario.

Pete Kilduff, the second baseman, led off the Brooklyn fifth with a single and moved to second on catcher Otto Miller's single. And up came the pitcher, Clarence Mitchell. As hurlers go, Mitchell wasn't a bad hitter at all. The season before he had produced 18 hits in 49 at-bats for a robust .367 average. Realizing that Mitchell was a dangerous left-handed pull hitter, Wambsganss crept back on the grass. When Mitchell hit a Bagby fastball on a line up the middle, Wambsganss threw himself at the ball—and caught it. Kilduff, assuming the ball was headed for center field, was nearly into third when Wambsganss stepped on second to double him up. Turning quickly toward first, the second baseman spotted Miller standing just a few feet away, frozen in his tracks. Wambsganss made two short steps to his left and tagged Miller on the shoulder. One, two, three. Wambsganss had turned the only unassisted triple play in World Series history.

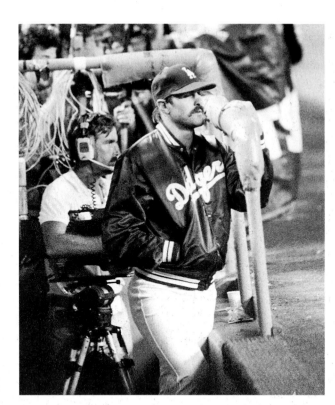

*Kirk Harold Gibson (left) waits in the wings for a chance to swing at the ball during the 1988 World Series. Moments later Gibson swats a dramatic home run and triumphantly tours the bases (opposite page) despite a ravaged left hamstring.*

# Gibson's Heroic Swing

Scan the list of World Series Most Valuable Player and you will find some larger-than-life names: Whitey Ford, Bob Gibson, Brooks Robinson, Roberto Clement, Reggie Jackson, Mike Schmidt, and Jack Morris. One name you will not find is Kirk Harold Gibson. Too bad, because with one swing, with a single at-bat, he probably changed the course of the 1988 World Series.

The Los Angeles Dodgers were a proud franchise, but they slipped in the mid-1980s. In 1987, they were last in the majors in hitting and runs scored. They were, on balance, fairly pathetic. In 1988, everything fell back into place. The pitching developed nicely, the hitting wasn't overpowering, but it was good enough to help the Dodgers win the National League West with a record of 94-67. Still, they were heavy underdogs to the Oakland Athletics in the World Series. The A's had won 104 games, and some people wondered aloud if the Dodgers were the worst team in history to reach the ultimate series. The Dodgers themselves quietly bit their lips.

It all unfolded true to form in Game One. The A's found themselves with a 4-3 lead with two out in the ninth inning and their ace reliever, Dennis Eckersley, on the mound with the anonymous Dave Anderson coming to the plate. With Mike Davis on first base, the recipient of a rare walk from Eckersley, manager Tommy Lasorda played his trump card. Moments

earlier, in the dead silence of the Dodgers' clubhouse, Gibson had been lying on the trainer's table watching the game on television. When an NBC commentator suggested that Gibson's bruised right knee and ravaged left hamstring would prevent the outfielder from playing in the opening game, he cursed and limped to the batting cage under the stands. Gibson sent word to Lasorda that he wanted to pinch-hit if a situation presented itself. And so it did.

When Davis drew ball four, Gibson came hobbling up the runway to the dugout, and Lasorda had no choice. He recalled Anderson and the crowd buzzed. Eckersley pushed Gibson into a 2-2 hole, and it appeared that the batter, clearly uncomfortable at the plate, would fail. Gibson spoiled the potential third strike three times with foul balls. The next pitch darted just outside the strike zone, leaving the count full and the atmosphere charged. Eckersley did not want to give Gibson anything too good, so he send a slider toward the dirt. It was over the plate, though, and Gibson golfed it five rows into the bleachers in right field. It was almost painful to watch as Gibson dragged himself around the bases, pumping his fists. It was a dramatic home run, one of the most breathtaking in World Series history. The Dodgers won the game on the strength of Gibson's only plate appearance. And though Orel Hershiser won a pair of games against the A's—one a three-hitter, the other a four-hitter in the deciding fifth game—it was Gibson who made it all possible.

# BASEBALL LEGENDS CHRONOLOGY

**1876** • *The National League is formed on February 2.*

**1880** • *The Cincinnati franchise is thrown out of the league for serving liquor in the stands and playing on Sunday.*

**1901** • *The American League is formed.*

**1903** • *16,242 witness the first World Series game on October 1, between the Boston Red Sox and Pittsburgh Pirates. The Pirates win, 7-3, but drop the series in seven games.*

**1909** • *National League President Harry C. Pulliam has a nervous breakdown and kills himself with a pistol on July 29.*

**1912** • *Ty Cobb is suspended on May 15 for jumping into the grandstands and fighting a fan. His teammates refuse to play until the suspension is lifted, forcing the Detroit front office to gather an impromptu team to play the Philadelphia Athletics. The one-day major leaguers lose, 23-2. Cobb is reinstated on May 26.*

**1916** • *For the first time in ten years, Ty Cobb (.371) loses the American League batting title; Tris Speaker (.386) ends his unprecedented dominance.*

**1919** • *The Chicago White Sox throw the World Series to the Cincinnati Reds. Scandal erupts. Within a year, eight White Sox players are barred from the major leagues forever.*

**1920** • *Cleveland's Ray Chapman is hit by Yankee pitcher Carl May's fastball, and dies the next day, thus becoming the first and only fatality of major league baseball.*

**1925** • *Babe Ruth is fined a record $5,000 for insubordination and breaking club training rules.*

*• The Baseball Hall of Fame in Cooperstown, New York, is founded. Ty Cobb is its first inductee.*

1941 • Joe DiMaggio hits safely in 56 consecutive games.

1945 • The St. Louis Browns sign Pete Gray, a one-armed outfielder.

1947 • Jackie Robinson becomes the first black player in the major leagues.

1949 • Philadelphia Philly Eddie Waitkus is shot in the lung by a deranged fan who lured him to her hotel room in Chicago. "If I couldn't have him, neither could anybody else," she later says. Waitkus recovers and continues to play.

1951 • Topps introduces the first baseball card. It is packed with caramel candy instead of gum.

1953 • On May 6, the St. Louis Browns' "Bobo" Holloman becomes the first pitcher to throw a no-hitter in his debut in the majors. By July 23, the 3-7 Bobo is sent back to the minor leagues, never to play in the majors again.

1955 • Cy Young and Honus Wagner die within a month of each other.

1956 • Don Larsen pitches the first no-hitter in a World Series.

1957 • The Brooklyn Dodgers and the New York Giants both decide to relocate to California.

1958 • Dodger Roy Campanella is paralyzed in a Long Island auto accident, ending his career.

1958 • For the first time, a World Series game is played completely under lights.

**1961** • *Roger Maris hits 61 home runs, in a 162-game season (which is eight games more than the traditional 154-game season), breaking Babe Ruth's record amid controversy. Maris enters the record books with an asterisk as a result.*

**1964** • *The Boyer family is divided about the World Series: Ken Boyer plays third base for the St. Louis Cards; brother Clete is at third for the opposing Yankees.*

**1965** • *The free agent draft becomes a reality. Nineteen-year-old Arizona State University outfielder Rick Monday is reportedly paid $100,000 to sign with the Kansas City Athletics.*

**1966** • *Artificial turf is introduced to baseball. Philly Dick Allen sums up the purists' opinion with, "I don't want to play on any grass a cow wouldn't eat."*

**1967** • *Denny McClain injures two toes chasing raccoons, he says, and is sidelined. Later,* Sports Illustrated *contends that McClain's injury was caused by a mob leader in response to gambling debts. Three years later Bowie Kuhn suspends him for "bookmaking activities in 1967 and associations at the time."*

**1969** • *The All-Star game is rained out for the first time.*

**1970** • *While on the witness stand in a case brought by Curt Flood of the Phillies, which challenged baseball's Reserve Clause, player-turned-broadcaster Joe Garagiola tells the judge, "I wish you were on a baseball card. I'd have you."*

**1971** • *On June 23, Rick Wise of the Phillies pitches a no-hitter. He also hits two home runs.*

**1972** • *The first player strike in baseball history begins on April 1, ending 13 days later.*

**1973** • *The designated hitter is introduced.*

**1973** • *George Steinbrenner buys the Yankees, saying "I look forward to coming to town just to see the games... We plan absentee ownership."*

**1974** • *The Cleveland Indians declare their June 4 contest against the Texas Indians "Beer Night," during which fans can get a cup of beer for just 10 cents. Fights break out in the stands, firecrackers are thrown in the Rangers' dugout, and in the ninth inning, fans storm the field. The Indians forfeit the game.*

**1975** • *0-2 pitcher Burt Hooton is traded from the Cubs to the Dodgers. He winds up with 18 victories.*

*1976* • *Twenty-two-year-old Detroit pitcher Mark Fidrych emerges as the year's phenomenon. He talks to the ball before throwing, flaps his arms on the mound (thus earning the nickname "Big Bird"), and ends the season with a 19-9 record, leading the league in complete games and ERA.*

*1977* • *Players' salaries jump 45 percent in one year. The Yankees raise their upper grandstand admission price from $1.50 to $4.50.*

*1978* • *Dodger pitcher Don Sutton, long suspected of doctoring the ball, gets the last laugh when an umpire checks Sutton's glove for foreign substances and instead finds a note which reads, "You're getting warm, but it's still not here."*

*1979* • *The June 12 Chicago-Detroit doubleheader is labeled Disco Demolition Night, in which fans bringing a disco record to be burned between games are admitted for 98 cents. Between games bases are torn up, fires are set, and 37 fans arrested. Chicago forfeits the second game.*

*1981* • *The Major League Players Association strikes for 50 days in the summer. The cost? Fans are openly hostile, 713 games are missed, and an estimated $98 million in revenue is lost.*

*1982* • *The Atlanta Braves win their first 13 games of the season, a record. Later, they remove a teepee of their mascot, Chief Noc-A-Homa, from the left field stands, and quickly drop 15 of the next 16 games. The teepee then returns.*

*1983* • *On July 24 George Brett hits a two-run homer in the ninth inning against the Yankees, but it is found that pine tar, on the bat for a better grip, was higher than the rulebook allowed. The runs are nullified. Kansas City protests, the runs are reinstated, and a date set for the play to resume. Tempers flare, and George Steinbrenner is fined $250,000 by Bowie Kuhn for "certain public statements" regarding the incident.*

*1983* • *Yankee center fielder Dave Winfield accidentally throws a ball at a sea gull during a game with Toronto, killing the bird. Winfield is arrested by Toronto police, and fined $500 for "willfully causing unnecessary cruelty to animals." The charges are eventually dropped.*

*1985* • *Former Philadelphia Phillies' clubhouse caterer Curtis Strong is convicted of selling cocaine to a variety of baseball players.*

*1987* • *A cheating epidemic resurfaces. Pitcher Joe Niekro is suspended for carrying an emery board in his back pocket; various players are accused of corking their bats. Commissioner Peter Ueberroth decrees that teams will be permitted to impound one bat belonging to an opponent per game.*

*1991* • *Outfielder Bobby Bonilla signs a five-year, $29 million contract with the New York Mets. His average yearly salary of $5.8 million surpasses the previous record, $5.3 million by pitcher Roger Clemens of the Boston Red Sox.*

*1992* • *Atlanta pitcher Tom Glavine, carries a 13-3 record into the All-Star Game. He is honored as the starting pitcher, but he gets shelled. Glavine allows nine hits and five runs in less than two innings—an All-Star Game record. His earned run average for the night is 27.0.*

# HALL OF FAME MEMBERS

The first number in parenthesis indicates the total number of votes possible in a given year. The numbers in parenthesis next to a player's name indicates the amount of votes received. (To be inducted, a player must receive at least 75 percent of the total possible votes.) Members with no corresponding numbers have been inducted by special committee. An asterisk (*) indicates a member who was selected as a non-player.

**1936** Total votes (226)
Ty Cobb (222)
Honus Wagner (215)
Babe Ruth (215)
Christy Mathewson (205)
Walter Johnson (189)

**1937** Total votes (201)
Nap Lajoie (168)
Tris Speaker (165)
Cy Young (153)
*Morgan B. Bulkeley
*Ban Johnson
Connie Mack
John McGraw
George Wright

**1938** Total votes (262)
Pete Alexander (212)
*Alexander Cartwright
*Henry Chadwick

**1939** Total votes (274)
George Sisler (235)
Eddie Collins (213)
Willie Keeler (207)
Lou Gehrig (by special election)
Cap Anson
Charlie Comiskey
Candy Cummings
Buck Ewing
Hoss Radbourne
Al Spalding

**1942**
Rogers Hornsby (182)

**1944**
*Judge Kenesaw M. Landis

**1945**
Roger Bresnahan
Dan Brouthers
Fred Clarke
Jimmie Collins
Ed Delahanty
Hugh Duffy
Hughie Jennings
Mike Kelly
Jim O'Rourke
Wilbert Robinson

**1946**
Jesse Burkett
Frank Chance
Jack Chesbro
Johnny Evers
Clark Griffith
Tom McCarthy
Joe McGinnity
Eddie Plank
Joe Tinker
Rube Waddell
Ed Walsh

**1947** Total votes (161)
Carl Hubbell (140)
Frank Frisch (136)
Mickey Cochrane (128)
Lefty Grove (123)

**1948** Total votes (121)
Herb Pennock (94)
Pie Traynor (93)

**1949** Total votes (187)
Charlie Gehringer (159)
Three-Finger Brown
Kid Nichols

**1951** Total votes (226)
Mel Ott (197)
Jimmie Foxx (179)

**1952** Total votes (234)
Harry Heilmann (203)
Paul Waner (195)

**1953** Total votes (264)
Dizzy Dean (209)
Al Simmons (199)
*Ed Barrow
Chief Bender
*Tom Connolly
*Bill Klem
Bobby Wallace
*Harry Wright

**1954** Total votes (252)
Rabbit Maranville (209)
Bill Dickey (202)
Bill Terry (195)

**1955** Total votes (251)
Joe DiMaggio (223)
Ted Lyons (217)
Dazzy Vance (205)
Gabby Hartnett (195)
Frank Baker
Ray Schalk

**1956** Total votes (193)
Hank Greenberg (164)
Joe Cronin (152)

**1957**
Sam Crawford
*Joe McCarthy

**1959**
Zack Wheat

**1961**
Max Carey
Billy Hamilton

**1962** Total votes (160)
Bob Feller (150)
Jackie Robinson (124)
*Bill McKechnie
Edd Roush

**1963**
John Clarkson
Elmer Flick
Sam Rice
Eppa Rixey

**1964** Total votes (225)
Luke Appling (189)
Red Faber
Burleigh Grimes
*Miller Huggins
Tim Keefe
Heinie Manush
John Ward

**1965**
Pud Galvin

**1966** Total votes (302)
Ted Williams (282)
*Casey Stengel

**1967** Total votes (306)
Red Ruffing (266)
*Branch Rickey
Lloyd Waner

**1968** Total votes (283)
Joe Medwick (240)
Kiki Cuyler
Goose Goslin

**1969** Total Votes (340)
Stan Musial (317)
Roy Campanella (270)
Stan Coveleski
Waite Hoyt

**1970** Total votes (300)
Lou Boudreau (232)
Earle Combs
*Ford Frick
Jesse Haines

**1971**
Jake Beckley
Dave Bancroft
Chick Hafey
Harry Hooper
Joe Kelley
Rube Marquard
*George Weiss
Satchel Paige

**1972** Total votes (396)
Sandy Koufax (344)
Yogi Berra (339)
Early Wynn (301)
Lefty Gomez
*Will Harridge
Ross Youngs
Josh Gibson
Buck Leonard

**1973** Total votes (380)
Warren Spahn (316)
*Billy Evans
George Kelly
Mickey Welch
Monte Irvin
Special waiver of
5-year waiting period:
Roberto Clemente

**1974** Total votes (365)
Mickey Mantle (322)
Whitey Ford (284)
Jim Bottomley
*Jocko Conlan
Sam Thompson
Cool Papa Bell

**1975** Total votes (362)
Ralph Kiner (273)
Earl Averill
*Buckey Harris
Billy Herman
Judy Johnson

| 1976 | Total votes (388) | 1987 | Total votes (413) |
|------|-------------------|------|-------------------|

1976 Total votes (388)
Robin Roberts (337)
Bob Lemon (305)
Roger Connor
Fred Lindstrom
*Cal Hubbard
Oscar Charleston

1977 Total votes (383)
Ernie Banks (321)
Amos Rusie
Joe Sewell
*Al Lopez
Martin Dihigo
John Henry Lloyd

1978 Total votes (379)
Eddie Mathews (310)
Addie Joss
*Larry MacPhail

1979 Total votes (432)
Willie Mays (409)
*Warren Giles
Hack Wilson

1980 Total votes (385)
Al Kaline (340)
Duke Snider (333)
Chuck Klein
*Tom Yawkey

1981 Total votes (401)
Bob Gibson (337)
Johnny Mize
Rube Foster

1982 Total votes (415)
Hank Aaron (406)
Frank Robinson (370)
Travis Jackson
*Happy Chandler

1983 Total votes (374)
Brooks Robisnon (344)
Juan Marichal (313)
George Kell
*Walt Alston

1984 Total votes (403)
Luis Aparicio (341)
Harmon Killebrew (335)
Don Drysdale (316)
Rick Ferrell
Pee Wee Reese

1985 Total votes (395)
Hoyt Wilhelm (331)
Lou Brock (315)

1986 Total votes (425)
William McCovey (346)
Bobby Doerr
Ernie Lombardi

1987 Total votes (413)
Billy Williams (354)
Catfish Hunter (315)
Ray Dandridge

1988 Total votes (427)
William Stargell (352)

1989 Total votes (447)
Johnny Bench (431)
Carl Yastrzemski (423)

1990 Total votes (444)
Jim Palmer (411)
Joe Morgan (363)

1991 Total votes (443)
Rod Carew (401)
Gaylord Perry (342)
Ferguson Jenkins (334)

1992 Total votes (430)
Tom Seaver (425)
Rollie Fingers (349)

# MOST VALUABLE PLAYER AWARD WINNERS

as voted by the Baseball Writers' Association

| National League | American League |
|-----------------|-----------------|
| 1931 Frank Frisch, St. Louis | 1931 Lefty Grove, Philadelphia |
| 1932 Charles Klein, Philadelphia | 1932 Jimmy Foxx, Philadelphia |
| 1933 Carl Hubbell, New York | 1933 Jimmy Foxx, Philadelphia |
| 1934 Dizzy Dean, St. Louis | 1934 Mickey Cochrane, Detroit |
| 1935 Gabby Hartnett, Chicago | 1935 Henry Greenberg, Detroit |
| 1936 Carl Hubbell, New York | 1936 Lou Gehrig, New York |
| 1937 Joe Medwick, St. Louis | 1937 Charley Gehringer, Detroit |
| 1938 Ernie Lombardi, Cincinnati | 1938 Jimmy Foxx, Boston |
| 1939 Buckey Walters, Cincinnati | 1939 Joe DiMaggio, New York |
| 1940 Frank McCormick, Cincinnati | 1940 Hank Greenberg, Detroit |
| 1941 Dolph Camilli, Brooklyn | 1941 Joe DiMaggio, New York |
| 1942 Mort Cooper, St. Louis | 1942 Joe Gordon, New York |
| 1943 Stan Musial, St. Louis | 1943 Spurgeon Chandler, New York |
| 1944 Martin Marion, St. Louis | 1944 Hal Newhouser, Detroit |
| 1945 Phil Cavarretta, Chicago | 1945 Hal Newhouser, Detroit |
| 1946 Stan Musial, St. Louis | 1946 Ted Williams, Boston |
| 1947 Bob Elliott, Boston | 1947 Joe DiMaggio, New York |
| 1948 Stan Musial, St. Louis | 1948 Lou Boudreau, Cleveland |
| 1949 Jackie Robinson, Brooklyn | 1949 Ted Williams, Boston |
| 1950 Jim Konstanty, Philadelphia | 1950 Phil Rizzuto, New York |
| 1951 Roy Campanella, Brooklyn | 1951 Yogi Berra, New York |
| 1952 Hank Sauer, Chicago | 1952 Bobby Shantz, Philadelphia |
| 1953 Roy Campanella, Brooklyn | 1953 Al Rosen, Cleveland |
| 1954 Willie Mays, New York | 1954 Yogi Berra, New York |
| 1955 Roy Campanella, Brooklyn | 1955 Yogi Berra, New York |
| 1956 Don Newcombe, Brooklyn | 1956 Mickey Mantle, New York |
| 1957 Henry Aaron, Milwaukee | 1957 Mickey Mantle, New York |
| 1958 Ernie Banks, Chicago | 1958 Jackie Jensen, Boston |
| 1959 Ernie Banks, Chicago | 1959 Nellie Fox, Chicago |
| 1960 Dick Groat, Pittsburgh | 1960 Roger Maris, New York |
| 1961 Frank Robinson, Cincinnati | 1961 Roger Maris, New York |
| 1962 Maury Wills, Los Angeles | 1962 Mickey Mantle, New York |
| 1963 Sandy Koufax, Los Angeles | 1963 Elston Howard, New York |
| 1964 Ken Boyer, St. Louis | 1964 Brooks Robinson, Baltimore |
| 1965 Willie Mays, San Francisco | 1965 Zoila Versailles, Minnesota |
| 1966 Roberto Clemente, Pittsburgh | 1966 Frank Robinson, Baltimore |
| 1967 Orlando Cepeda, St. Louis | 1967 Carl Yastrzemski, Boston |
| 1968 Bob Gibson, St. Louis | 1968 Denny McClain, Detroit |
| 1969 Willie McCovey, San Francisco | 1969 Harmon Killebrew, Minnesota |
| 1970 Johnny Bench, Cincinnati | 1970 John (Boog) Powell, Baltimore |
| 1971 Joe Torre, St. Louis | 1971 Vida Blue, Oakland |
| 1972 Johnny Bench, Cincinnati | 1972 Dick Allen, Chicago |
| 1973 Pete Rose, Cincinnati | 1973 Reggie Jackson, Oakland |
| 1974 Steve Garvey, Los Angeles | 1974 Jeff Burroughs, Texas |
| 1975 Joe Morgan, Cincinnati | 1975 Fred Lynn, Boston |
| 1976 Joe Morgan, Cincinnati | 1976 Thurman Munson, New York |
| 1977 George Foster, Cincinnati | 1977 Rod Carew, Minnesota |
| 1978 Dave Parker, Pittsburgh | 1978 Jim Rice, Boston |
| 1979 (tie)Willie Stargell, Pittsburgh | 1979 Don Baylor, California |
|     Keith Hernandez, St. Louis | 1980 George Brett, Kansas City |
| 1980 Mike Schmidt, Philadelphia | 1981 Rollie Fingers, Milwaukee |
| 1981 Mike Schmidt, Philadelphia | 1982 Robin Yount, Milwaukee |
| 1982 Dale Murphy, Atlanta | 1983 Cal Ripken Jr., Baltimore |
| 1983 Dale Murphy, Atlanta | 1984 Willie Hernandez, Detroit |
| 1984 Ryne Sandberg, Chicago | 1985 Don Mattingly, New York |
| 1985 Willie McGee, St. Louis | 1986 Roger Clemens, Boston |
| 1986 Mike Schmidt, Philadelphia | 1987 George Bell, Toronto |
| 1987 Andre Dawson, Chicago | 1988 Jose Canseco, Oakland |
| 1988 Kirk Gibson, Los Angeles | 1989 Robin Yount, Milwaukee |
| 1989 Kevin Mitchell, San Francisco | 1990 Rickey Henderson, Oakland |
| 1990 Barry Bonds, Pittsburgh | 1991 Cal Ripken, Jr., Baltimore |
| 1991 Terry Pendleton, Atlanta | 1992 Dennis Eckersley, Oakland |
| 1992 Barry Bonds, Pittsburgh | |

# USEFUL ADDRESSES

Baseball Commissioner's Office
350 Park Ave.
New York, NY 10022

**National League**

National League Office
350 Park Ave.
New York, NY 10022

Atlanta Braves
PO Box 4064
Atlanta, GA 30302

Chicago Cubs
Wrigley Field
Chicago, IL 60613

Cincinnati Reds
100 Riverfront Stadium
Cincinnati, OH 45202

Denver Rockies
1700 Broadway
Denver, CO 80290

Florida Marlins
100 NE Third Ave.
Ft. Lauderdale, FL 33301

Houston Astros
Astrodome
Houston, TX 77001

Los Angeles Dodgers
Dodger Stadium
Los Angeles, CA 90012

Montreal Expos
PO Box 500, Station M
Montreal, PQ H1V 3P2

New York Mets
Shea Stadium
Flushing, NY 11368

Philadelphia Phillies
PO Box 7575
Philadelphia, PA 19101

Pittsburgh Pirates
Three Rivers Stadium
Pittsburgh, PA 15212

St. Louis Cardinals
Busch Stadium
St. Louis, MO 63102

San Diego Padres
PO Box 2000
San Diego, CA 92120

San Francisco Giants
Candlestick Park
San Francisco, CA 04124

**American League**

American League Office
350 Park Ave.
New York, NY 10022

Baltimore Orioles
633 W. Camden St.
Baltimore, MD 21201

Boston Red Sox
24 Yawkey Way
Boston, MA 02215

California Angels
Anaheim Stadium
Anaheim, CA 92806

Chicago White Sox
333 W. 35th St.
Chicago, IL 60616

Cleveland Indians
Cleveland Stadium
Cleveland, OH 44114

Detroit Tigers
Tiger Stadium
Detroit, MI 48216

Kansas City Royals
Harry S. Truman Sports
   Complex
Kansas City, MO 64141

Milwaukee Brewers
Milwaukee County Stadium
Milwaukee, WI 53214

Minnesota Twins
501 Chicago Ave. South
Minneapolis, MN 55415

New York Yankees
Yankee Stadium
Bronx, NY 10451

Oakland A's
Oakland Coliseum
Oakland, CA 94621

Seattle Mariners
100 S. King St.
Seattle, WA 98104

Texas Rangers
1200 Copeland Rd.
Arlington, TX 76011

Toronto Blue Jays
Box 7777
Adelaide St. PO
Toronto, ON M5C 2K7

# INDEX